in the rearview mirror

LEE LIVINGSTON

www.intherearviewmirrorbook.com
Cover illustration and design by David Ensz

For Linda, Tim and Joey
and in memory of Robert T. Lyons Jr.
and Robert Lehmann

"I don't know how 'great' America was a while back,
but it sure as hell was a lot more friendly!"

– Overheard old timer speaking at a Cleveland Indians spring training game in Goodyear, Arizona, March 2017.

CHAPTER 1

Sequoia

A best friend in high school is a friend for life, except when he shoots himself at twenty-nine.

The first time I had a clue Dango might be a little crazy was when he threatened to throw himself off Moro Rock back at Sequoia National Park in the summer of 1961. That was not some idle threat he was going to jump and just stub a toe. No, that was going to be a leap into oblivion.

Moro Rock proudly juts out from the park of giant trees high in the Sierras. A massive promontory of bare granite with a quarter-mile footpath of steps and handrails carved into it so visitors can climb up to its peak viewing point. There, looking to the west out over the foothills and the Kaweah River canyon below, you can make out the dirty haze of the endless San Joaquin Valley. Looking to the east, the highest mountains in the Western Divide are so close they almost reach out and smack you. Snow-capped Mount Whitney, front and center.

If you looked down, well, there was just no point in looking down;

you couldn't make out the canyon floor past Moro's sheer slope. I just knew it was over 6,000 feet until you hit something, and after 6,000 feet it wouldn't make any difference what you hit. Yet, here I was, at dusk, on that late July day, actually worrying about the drop-off from Moro Rock because my big lug of a best friend had climbed under the guardrail and was now standing, back pressed spread-eagle against the slope, arguing with me.

"We've got to go back home," he said.

"Bob," I replied. Dango was his high school nickname. I only used his real name when we were fighting. "When you get back on this side of the rail we'll talk about it."

"I will," he said. "When you agree to go back to Cleveland next week."

A grown-up would have left him there and called his bluff. I, on the other hand, a very mature 18-year-old, leaned back, took a sip from the one remaining beer in our Hamm's six-pack, and wondered what I was going to do to handle this bizarre situation. 'Cause, truth be told, I wanted to go back to Cleveland, too. I just wanted to figure a way to do it without getting killed by my dad.

The reason the two of us were perched on that granite dome in the Sierras and not sweltering away in Cleveland humidity was because of my father. He knew somebody in Washington, D.C. and had pulled strings to get us the summer jobs of a lifetime working in a national park. Dango and I had even driven down to D.C. over Christmas break to seal the deal. We met the gentleman in his gray Department of Interior office and presented ourselves with sports coats and ties to show him we were upstanding young college-bound men. Perfect for stocking the shelves, unloading trucks and running the ice house at the Sequoia Village Market. The meeting lasted about 45 minutes. We stressed how much we really wanted the jobs; he talked about what a good experience it would be for us and how he didn't like the Cleveland Browns. Not one word was said about giant sequoias, nature or the environment.

Two days after graduation from University School, Cleveland's finest all-male prep school, Dango and I had loaded up my '56 black-and-red Pontiac Star Chief convertible and headed out for California. What a ride! Top down, radio up and a cold brew here and there when we could see for miles and be sure to spot the Highway Patrol. We alternated driving and pulled off the highway for catnaps. No stopping to spend the night. We were in a hurry because we were 18. Food was beer, coffee, burgers and candy bars. The country flew by in a blur of cornfields, wheat fields and silos, gas stations, overpasses and Burma Shave rhymes. *"If daisies are your favorite flowers keep pushin' up those miles per hour!"* And boy did we push that powerful Pontiac V-8. The Star Chief barreled down the straight-aways and hugged every curve like a racer. How could it not help but hug the highway with a wheelbase close to six-by-eleven feet and a curb weight of over 3,700 pounds. Daisies were the furthest things from our minds. We had decades to go before we slept. We were two privileged, white, American boys on the road to California and points beyond.

"Come on, Lee," Dango bellowed from the slope. "We don't go back now, we're gonna miss it all. The last summer we'll all be together."

"Getting tired?" I answered. "Don't make any quick moves."

After my attempt at sarcasm, I looked at him, perched over the void and I began to understand our close friendship. We were made for each other. He was always impulsive and a little crazy. I thought things out too much and played it way too safe. He pushed and when he went too far, I pulled him back. I also knew at that point that I'd bring him back from Moro Rock and he'd get me to go back to Cleveland. His next question cinched it.

"In 20 years will it make a difference?" he asked.

"What?" I said, not knowing where he was going.

"You think your dad, or the guys at the market, or anyone for that matter, will give a damn that we cut out on the jobs early any more than a couple of weeks after we do it?" he said.

"What's that got to do with 20 years?" I replied.

"Just taking it to the extreme to make a point," he said.

He had me and I knew it. I knew that if we left after only a month of work my dad would blow his stack and then forget about it in a week. The manager of the Sequoia Village Market would be upset with the inconvenience and then hire some friend's kids from Visalia. And the guy in the gray office in Washington, he wouldn't even hear about it. "In 20 years will it make a difference?" became our motto, our battle cry. What a great credo for teenagers to justify anything they wanted to do. Dango and I used it often that summer as we embarked on an adventure and did things we'd never do again. We cut ourselves loose, gave ourselves our freedom, because we knew, with the certainty of 18-year-old's, that in 20 years nothing we did would make any difference. It was a lie, of course. At least for me.

"Okay, get over here," I shouted. "We'll go back next week. Let's just figure out how."

"Hatta boy!" he exclaimed, lunging for the guardrail. How he got any traction off that rock, I'll never know, but he was able to catch the rail with one hand, and then my hand with his other. Pulling together, we got his 6'2", 190-pound frame back over to safety.

 Fifty years later, whenever I look back, I always see that early evening on Moro Rock as the starting point: the starting point for the grand and strange adventure that was about to unfold. And, as the years pass, I am always looking back from further away and higher up, higher even than the Sierras, so I can see the entire journey before me. Sequoia at one end and Cleveland, the center of our 18-year-old universe, at the other. I see a country that was smaller and more open, people who were bigger and more open. I see the web of interstates just beginning to creep across the land. And, like most men of my age, I miss that time of my youth. But, most of all, I miss Dango full of life.

"Can I have the last swig of that beer?" he asked when he was standing next to me.

"Help yourself," I said, handing it to him. "Now, let's go. There's an employee dance at the rec center. Some of the girls from the lodge'll be there."

For someone who had just been on the verge of extinction, Dango, in the car on the short ride back to Sequoia Village, was a changed man. He had solved the one big problem on his mind and he now happily related all his many plans for Cleveland when we got back. That was one of the main reasons you had to love the big guy. No hidden agenda. He always told you what was on his mind. It's a trait I've always looked for in my male friends. It was easier to find then, not so easy now or since.

As for what we looked for in females? At that time, anything we could get. The 6'2" Dango had a great physique, brown thick wavy hair and no acne whatsoever. The thick horn-rimmed glasses might have been a little off-putting, but hey, this was way before the widespread use of contacts and lots of guys wore glasses. I was blonde, a half-inch under six feet. In the summer of '61, my hair had bleached out a little from all the sun and top-down driving. My white, white Anglo skin also had no acne because of the month's relatively clean outdoor California living and, because I was fair, I was hard-pressed to shave more than twice a week. I even sported a light golden T-shirt tan. A regular young Adonis, in my own mind.

We may have thought we looked pretty hot, but one reason we were so ready to head back to Cleveland was we'd already struck out with all the college and high school girls that worked at Sequoia. Our problem was not that we were unattractive; it was that we were foreign.

Most of the other kids working at Sequoia were from California. Apparently, out of the Sequoia workforce, only Dango and I had gone to the Department of the Interior to get our jobs from a "family friend." Most of the other employees had worked summers at Sequoia for years. They were "cool." They were more "laid back." They actually spoke another language, as I was soon to find out.

When we got to the lodge rec room, we headed over to a group of guys surrounding Joey Burkett, a U.C. Santa Barbara sophomore, and our immediate superior at the market. If you had to give his job a title, it would probably have been Assistant Manager, the highest position a summer employee could reach. Senior stock boy in charge of stock boys. He was definitely the coolest of the California guys. Very tan, close-cropped brown hair with sun-bleached highlights, and a great smile with teeth so white he could have been in an Ipana toothpaste ad. He was always at ease, and no wonder, his girlfriend worked in reservations at the lodge and had a room there. He did not have to sleep every night in a 12' by 12' barren cabin *"tossin' and turning"* like the summer's number one hit song. As his "market boys," he'd befriended us and taken us under his wing.

"Get over here, boys," Joey said as we approached. "Tonight's your lucky night. There's fresh meat in town."

He gestured for us to look over by the small table where Billy Pancetti was DJ'ing with a single record player and a large stack of 45s. Billy was not one of the "cooler" Californians. He was slight of build, shorter than I was by a good two inches and must have been from Northern Italian stock because he had long, stringy, blonde hair. He worked for park maintenance, driving one of those golf-cart-like scooters around the village to pick up and empty garbage. Despite being a glorified garbage collector, he smiled his way through every day and greeted everyone he met, tourist or fellow worker, with a friendly wave and "How ya doin'?"

Behind Billy were two older couples, married visitors I guessed, and "the meat," three girls with great tan legs which you couldn't help but notice since they were all wearing rolled-up jeans short shorts. The girls came in three sizes. The tallest of the three was a blonde with more than ample breasts accentuated in a tied-off men's madras shirt. The middle girl had striking blue eyes, streaked brown hair pulled back in a ponytail and a body that, in my 18-year-old estimation, was perfectly proportioned. The smaller girl, the longer you looked, was probably smaller because she was younger. She was a beauty, but had junior high school written all over her.

Joey had spotted these girls for Dango and me, precisely because they were younger and new. Dango certainly wasn't going to wait for me to make my move. First slow record Billy played, he headed straight toward the girl his size. Trouble was, so did just about every other horny male in that room. By the time he'd crossed over to where they were standing, the big one and the one I called "perfect" had been plucked and were already dancing. To not end up with egg on his face, he began dancing with the one whose head rested just above his navel. He looked over at me while they were dancing, easy to do since his chin could rest on her hair, and gave me one of those shit-eating, "what the hell" grins of his.

I just shook my head and smiled back at him. I knew exactly what he was thinking. He was not about to ask his petite partner her age. This was his first "bird in the hand" after four weeks in the forest. He was not letting go. Once my eyes left his and began to drift around the rest of the room, I immediately lost track of him, because my luck began to change. My "perfect" girl, while dancing with her partner, made eye contact with me and held it for a complete lyric line of *Crying* by Roy Orbison. In those days, and to an 18-year-old that hadn't kissed a girl for a month and a half, that was about as subtle a come on as a spoken "I want you." Next slow dance, I had her tight in my arms, and she looked up at me with those big, blue eyes.

"Are you a surfer?" she said.

Because I came from Cleveland and had no idea what a surfer was, I heard: "Are you a server?"

Always thinking fast, I replied quickly, "No, I work at the market." I could tell by the way her eyes widened, her mouth opened and her head tilted, that she didn't know where the hell that answer came from.

She tried again, "I didn't ask where you worked," she said. "I asked if you surfed."

Still on unsure ground, I answered, "No. Does that have something to do with swimming?"

She smiled. "You're not from California, are you?"

"No, I'm from Ohio," I said. Then, trying to pad my credentials, I added, "I'll be going to college out here in the fall."

"And you don't even know what surfing is, do you?" she asked, completely ignoring my reference to higher learning.

"No," I admitted.

"It's so bitchin'." She went on using another word I'd never heard. "The beaches, the sun, riding the waves. . . . You look like a surfer."

With that, she pushed herself harder into me and I knew that it was good to look like a surfer. When the dance ended, she lingered in my arms just long enough to extend an invitation.

"I could teach you to surf, if you came down to Long Beach," she said.

An hour after my decision to leave early and return to Cleveland, I regretted it. I'd just been offered the most beautiful initiation to becoming a Californian, but I was opting for Ohio.

No beach, no surf and, most definitely no body like the one walking away from me on the dance floor, awaited me there.

After two more dances, I learned that she was Billy Pancetti's sister, Barbara, and that she and her parents were returning to their home in Long Beach the next day. At 11:30, as the party was beginning to break up, Billy came over to where I was standing. Dango and the little one had disappeared, so I was worried that I was going to be facing the protective older brother without any backup. I should have known better.

"Hey Lee," Billy said. "Barbie really likes you. Maybe you can do me a big favor?"

"Sure," I answered.

Turns out the big favor he asked was if I could give him a ride down to Long Beach the coming weekend for a large Pancetti family get-together. Barb had suggested it, his parents had already approved. They even had a room for me in the garage behind their house. I could see Barb over Billy's shoulder looking at me with those big eyes and that coy smile. This was too good to be true – I could have a California weekend of surf and sex and still get to go back to Cleveland the next week. I accepted immediately and then talked to Joey to rearrange my weekend work schedule. We'd leave Saturday right after the early shift and come back for the late shift Monday.

When the dance ended for the evening, I walked over and met Billy and Barb's parents. They thanked me for agreeing to bring Billy down on Saturday and then headed back to their room. That left Barb there so she'd have a chance to say goodnight.

"Come on," Barb said taking my hand. "Walk me back to the lodge."

"Oh, brave new world," I thought to myself, remembering the novel from last summer's reading list, as we headed out. This was the California I'd imagined during those long Cleveland winters. The girls were tan, beautiful, and so advanced that they trained their parents to help them pick up the boy they wanted. Barb and I took the long way back to the lodge. She made it very clear that if I came to Long Beach, I would learn a lot more than just how to surf.

On the short walk back to Dango's and my cabin, I came up with a plan to make everything Dango and I wanted work out. Of course, it would require a few white lies. I'd take Billy to Long Beach, have my weekend as a surfer, and when I returned from the weekend, give the guys at the market some story about an emergency at home. Dango and I would be all broken up that we had to leave. We'd make our sincerest apologies and, by next week, we would be back on the road to Cleveland. We might not feel so good about ourselves, but no one would be the wiser.

Billy and I set off for Long Beach minutes after our Saturday shift ended at noon. It felt good to be on the road again. I went as fast as I could through the switchbacks heading down from Sequoia to the San Joaquin Valley. As we dropped, the temperature rose. When we hit the valley floor it was 110 degrees Fahrenheit. Didn't bother us, or the Star Chief. We just put the top down and let the wind keep us cool. As for the Pontiac, it showed no tendency to overheat as it purred along. I had the boys at the Sequoia Village Chevron change the oil and tune it up on Thursday. Everybody thought I had the service done for the trip to Long Beach; only Dango and I knew it was for the longer haul back to Cleveland.

By 1:00 p.m. we were on California Route 99 headed south. Route 99 was the main north/south highway through the San Joaquin – flat, straight as an arrow and never on anyone's list of scenic highways. Even in 1961, it was mostly four lanes. There were stretches with nothing but fields of crops on either side as far as you could see and where you could maintain speeds over 75. It was not an interstate with limited access. Roads would appear between the fields and you would never know when a slow truck filled with produce would suddenly cross or turn on in front of you. When you reached a town, they'd drop the speed limit from 65 to 25 and local cops were just waiting for red-and-black Pontiacs with Ohio plates. Billy had made the trip dozens of times, so he guided me through the speed traps. Soon we were out of Bakersfield and climbing the foothills at the south end of the valley. They called it the "Grapevine" then, and still do, but it must have gotten that name years before '61 because it was four lanes all the way and the curves and grade didn't faze the big Star Chief as we glided over.

By 3:15 p.m., we pulled off the Long Beach Freeway and I entered a whole new world. Long Beach turned out to be a revelation, in more ways than one. Every home we had passed on the way to the Pancetti's, in this neighborhood that seemed to go on forever, had been built in the last 10 to 15 years. The lots were all the same size. The houses looked to be all the same size. They were all one story and made with plaster or wood siding. These were "tract homes" and, just like the Pacific Ocean, I had never really seen them before.

Dango and I kept saying we were from Cleveland, but actually we were from the suburbs of Cleveland known as "The Heights." Shaker Heights and Cleveland Heights bordered the city of Cleveland to the east and, as the name suggests, were above the city that occupied the flatlands leading to Lake Erie. Many of the homes in the Heights were giant Tudors and brick colonials, surrounded by sprawling yards broken up with elegant, mature elms and sycamores. The homes had been built from the 1920s through the '40s during Cleveland's boom years as a great steel-manufacturing city. The streets in the Heights were never patterned in straight-line grids; they wound around and followed the contours of the land.

I guess it reeked of privilege, but I never thought of the Heights as an enclave of the rich. I did consider it, and myself, as "upper-middle class." Going to University School, however, Dango and I did have wealthy friends that lived in mansions. You knew they were definitely "rich" because they also had second homes down in Palm Beach where they went for semester and spring break.

Now, in a neighborhood over 2000 miles and what seemed like 100 years away from the Heights, I was getting a glimpse of a new and different way of life. An American family, very different from my own, was inviting me into their home to share their weekend, simply because I worked with their son and their daughter had taken a fancy to me. It was a display of openness and kindness that I had never experienced before. Certainly not in the Heights. I didn't know it then, but I would discover these same qualities quite often in the weeks ahead.

The other revelation about Long Beach was, despite Barb's perfect body and her willingness to share it, she bored me. Three hours talking with her and I was actually missing talking to Dango and making plans for the trip back. All she could manage to speak about was Long Beach and surfing.

We went to surf Friday night right next to a power plant, at a place called Seal Beach. The plant served a purpose because the waters next to it were nice and warm, and there was plenty of light so you could see what you were doing at night. The waves rolled in with a steady even cadence and not one of them topped four feet.

"It's perfect for a beginner," Barb said as we paddled out. She was on a smaller board she kept at home. I was on a board borrowed from one of Billy's friends.

I was pretty good at the paddling, but when it came to standing and riding a wave, that was another thing altogether. Barb finally gave up after about an hour and a half of trying to teach me. I had gotten to my feet at the most three times, and the longest distance I traveled before falling was maybe two board lengths. A little sore and beat up from constantly hitting the sandy bottom, I went back with Barb to warm up by the fire pit back on the beach. After a couple of beers and quite a few kisses, we were very warm. Barb picked up the blanket, took my hand and we headed away from the fire into the dark to get warmer.

Sex for an 18-year-old male in 1961 was never bad. After all, just getting to do the deed was a victory in itself. And I, for one, had little experience to measure it against, but Seal Beach does not rate a special place in my sexual highlights memory reel. With kids talking, laughing and throwing a Frisbee by the nearby fire pit and sand everywhere it shouldn't be, I was relieved when it was over. At least, I had accomplished my horny teenager goal and now I could concentrate on returning to Cleveland. The sooner the better.

Billy and I got back on the road early Monday morning. Even at 6:30 a.m. the traffic through LA was heavy. By the time we hit the San Joaquin valley it was 10:00 a.m. and the temperature was already in the 90s. We stopped at a Texaco truck stop, filled the tank, picked up a couple of Snickers bars and a Coors six-pack. We ate the Snickers and washed them down with our first two Coors while sitting in the parking lot. Before we left, we put the top down to keep cool.

Heading back up the 99 straightaway there was hardly a car in sight, so we decided to open our second beers. When we reached the Sequoia turn-off, Billy had stretched out on the Pontiac's big front seat and was getting a little shuteye after his hard night. Even now, so many years later, I remember that feeling of driving alone back to Sequoia: it was euphoric. Tomorrow Dango and I would tell our lie and start a new adventure. Today I could enjoy the last of this drive, top down, warm sun and the final switchbacks up the mountain to get back to the village on time.

The noise of tires on gravel woke me up. Feeling the bumpy off-road ride came a split second later. Then everything turned to slow motion. The road had made one of its many turns on the way up to Sequoia, and the Star Chief, driven by a happy sleeping teenager had continued straight ahead. Out the windshield was nothing but sky and mountains, not in front of me where they should have been, but off to my right where the road was. I locked my arms behind the steering wheel and looked down to my right as Billy fell off the front seat and bounced on the floor under the dashboard. Then the noise and bumpy ride stopped. We were airborne.

Looking back, I know it was fortunate that I had fallen asleep during the lower switchbacks. If I'd managed to stay awake to take the turns at a higher elevation, we might have dropped hundreds, even thousands of feet to a spectacular fiery death. The lower drive off into thin air was terrifying enough. The Pontiac saved us. It didn't nose down, or flip to the side. It continued straight and level, then, like Wiley Coyote in the Roadrunner cartoons, seemed to stop for a second in mid-air, then dropped straight down. Grasping the wheel and now wide-awake, I got to experience it all. I probably had the Coyote's stupid expression of resignation and doom on my face as I realized what I'd done and where I was headed. It turned out the drop was only 13 feet to a flat farm field cleared and ready for planting.

The Star Chief landed like the dead weight it was, perfectly upright, on all four tires. I bounced straight off my seat but held on to the steering wheel and came right back down. Billy was knocked off the floor and landed back in the passenger seat. It was a cartoon. The car kept going straight through a wood fence and finally stopped in the front yard of a farmhouse, four feet from a picture window. Billy and I were alright; the Pontiac even looked fine, just two guys parked in a convertible in an odd location.

The owner of the small farm and his wife rushed out of the house and up to the car. I expected to get a real tongue-lashing. All I got was kindness and concern.

"Are you boys okay?" he asked. "Anybody hurt?"

"I think we're both fine," I answered. "I think I fell asleep. We were on our way back to Sequoia. We work there."

"Come on out of the car and walk around a bit," he advised. "Make sure nothing's broken. I'll call the police and get a tow truck out here. After that drop, you've got to have some damage."

The word "police" got my brain going again. I whispered over to Billy as I opened the driver's side door, "Billy, find a bag or something and ditch the beer cans."

The close brush with death made Billy and me more alert. He finessed the beer can cleanup into a general car cleanup and found a trashcan by their garage to dump everything. The farm couple couldn't have been nicer. They gave us some soft drinks while we waited on the authorities. They also let me make a phone call up to the market. I got a hold of Joey Burkett and told him what happened. He assured me he'd find Dango and they would come right down to pick us up. We were only about 20 minutes from the park.

Nothing but good luck seemed to follow the accident. The cops showed up and since no one had been hurt and the owners didn't want to press any charges for damage to their field or fence, they shook their heads at our good fortune and left. They didn't even think to check us for alcohol. We'd gotten rid of the beer evidence and since we'd only had a couple we certainly weren't drunk; the brews had just helped us relax and fall asleep. The tow truck driver arrived shortly before Dango and Burkett. He checked out the Pontiac, had me start it, and pronounced it drivable. When Dango got there we started to drive it off the front lawn and noticed something dragging in the rear. He looked under the car and then opened the trunk. A two-by-four had broken off the fence and punctured through and into the trunk. Joey and Dango were able to pull it out from underneath and we jokingly presented it to the farm couple for firewood.

Billy decided to go back to Sequoia in Joey's car and I certainly understood since my driving had almost killed him. After they left, Dango got behind the wheel of the Pontiac and we headed up the farmer's long driveway back to the road I'd flown off just an hour or so earlier. I sat back in the passenger seat and took a deep sigh of relief. Despite the stupidity of my actions, Billy and I escaped with minimal damage. Dango and I were now free to proceed on our journey as we had planned and without another care in the world, the way it should be for soon-to-be college freshmen.

The driveway was paved, but definitely not highway-smooth. Where the fence crossed it there was an opening for the driveway to pass through and that's where we came to our first "bump in the road." It wasn't a large bump, but when we rolled over it Dango and I both lifted off the vinyl a good eight inches. The "after bumps" kept bouncing us until my faithful Star Chief hit the next bump on the road.

Dango, who knew way more about cars than I did, looked over at me:

"Shocks and suspension are totally shot. No way this car is making it back to Cleveland."

CHAPTER 2

Las Vegas

Dango and I waved goodbye to my brother Jay from the middle row seats of our Las Vegas bound Greyhound bus as it pulled out of the Hollywood station on Cahuenga Boulevard. Nothing had worked out the way I had planned. It was Sunday morning, one week less a day, since I had driven off the road on the way back up to Sequoia. We'd told our lies about having to leave, then made our apologies and farewells, packed up and started down the mountain on Thursday morning. We were headed to my older brother's house in the Hollywood Hills above Los Angeles. It was a very slow drive.

We kept the Star Chief in the right lane and never pushed it above 50. Even at the low speeds, every little bump lifted us off our seats. When other cars passed us, which was all the time, people would look over and laugh. That was really hard to take, especially when they were good-looking girls our age.

On Friday, we took the car to a Pontiac dealer near my brother's house and Dango's diagnosis was confirmed: The entire suspension would have to be replaced and that would cost more than the Star

Chief was worth. My father had only paid $750 to buy it used two years ago, just after my 16th birthday. Once I had my license, probably not a day had gone by that I hadn't driven the Pontiac somewhere: Every day to University School during the school year; with the top down during the Cleveland summers; with the top up, windows closed, heater blasting during the Cleveland winters. The car was part of me. I had hoped we could save it since it had saved me, but I knew my dad wouldn't hear of it. Later that night I made the dreaded call home to let the parents know what we had done. The phone call dealt with money, jobs and "responsibility," so it was definitely my dad's jurisdiction. Mom oversaw schoolwork and school-related issues. My dad had a hair-trigger temper and when I related all that had happened and that we wanted to come back to Cleveland I could feel his fury and disappointment from 2500 miles away. No screaming, no raising his voice, just bitter, clipped questions and statements.

"How much money have you got?"

"About $250 each," I answered. "The market paid us all they owed us when we left."

"The car's junk?" he said.

"Well the Pontiac dealer said maybe we could . . ." I started.

"The car's junk!" he interrupted. "Put Jay on the phone. I'll deal with you when you get back here."

I handed the phone to my brother and watched as he nodded and uttered a few "Yesses" and "Nos." He was getting orders. When he hung up, he turned to me and smiled. No matter the age difference between brothers, when one gets in trouble, the one that's not in trouble always seems to enjoy it.

"Whoa. That's as mad as I've heard him since I flunked out of Kenyon."

"Thanks for sticking up for me," I said. "Now what did he say?"

"Here's the deal: I sell the car here and whatever I get for it, I keep. You and Dango take the Greyhound back to Cleveland and pay for it yourselves."

"We can't fly?"

"Can you pay for it?" Jay asked. "No. You take the bus."

"Great," I sneered. "We'll leave tomorrow."

I sat back in the Greyhound, as the bus turned onto the Hollywood Freeway, still angry with my father and brother. I had practically cried when I said goodbye to the Star Chief, which I had left parked on the street in front of Jay's house. How could they take my first car away from me? How could they punish me for being completely irresponsible? I closed my eyes as the Greyhound settled into its steady cruising speed of 65 mph and started to drift off into memories of the Pontiac and all the good times it had made possible for Dango and me in Cleveland: The after-school jaunts out to the Chagrin River for talks and a six-pack; the return to Cleveland from our trip to D.C., fighting and laughing through a blizzard on the Pennsylvania Turnpike; double-dating at the old Mayfield drive-in theater. But it was one late summer night after our junior year that I recalled most vividly. It was the night Dango got his name.

I pulled the Star Chief to the side of North Park Boulevard near Roxboro Road and stopped. It was 1:30 a.m. on a Friday night/ Saturday morning in late July. Dango was with me; we'd just dropped our dates off in Shaker Heights and I was taking him home. Earlier, there had been one of those violent summer thunderstorms, but it was peaceful and quiet now. The rain had stopped; steam rose from the boulevard. Above, the leaves of the giant cedars and elms glistened in patches from the light of street lamps. I released the latches over the windshield to free the convertible top. Dango hopped out to pull the top back and stow it behind the backseat. We were going to have a last beer and review the evening.

The place was comfortable and familiar to us even at that late hour. Our old junior high school was just at the corner of Roxboro. The school was where we'd met and become friends, before being accepted to University School. To our right sat some of the oldest, largest and most expensive homes in Cleveland Heights, all dark except for an occasional hall or door light. To our left ran the North Park Ravine, dense with trees and foliage, completely wild, the dividing line between Cleveland Heights and Shaker Heights.

We were drinking Schafer's that night. "The one beer to have when you're having more than one." I loved that ad line. Beers were our vice during high school. No drugs, no marijuana – hadn't even heard of them yet. Only a few guys would drink hard liquor, but not any of our close friends. Beer was our release, our rebellion and we almost always had "more than one." Dango opened them with the can opener I kept in the glove compartment. The pointed end pierced the can, which then came to life with that familiar "swoosh" sound. We even had a nickname for the opener; we called it "the church key." Dango passed me my open can and I opened the questioning.

"What was it Jerome called you tonight?"

"Beaudango," he replied. "All the guys at the warehouse have picked it up."

That evening was the first I had ever heard the two syllables "dang-go." He was working for the second summer in a row at a metals warehouse in East Cleveland. I was working my first summer at a small machine shop out of town by the new interstate. Dango and I may have been upper-middle class boys from University School, but our dads both insisted that we work during the summers to earn our spending money. My dad put it best: "You work in places like this and you'll know why you want to go to college." He was right.

Almost all the other laborers at the warehouse where Dango worked were black. Jerome was one of those guys. He and Dango had become good friends. In fact, most of the workers there became his friends. They loved him for the same reason I did: no bullshit.

He told you what he thought and it was always honest. Of course, they liked him for other reasons too – he was strong, worked like an ox and would try anything once. Drinking beer and laughing at their stories didn't hurt either. And so began the evolution of a nickname, because blacks used nicknames for everyone way before prep school boys adopted the habit. When Dango first went to work at the warehouse they called him "Beauregard" – which was probably because he came off a little cocky so they'd slapped him with the name of a dapper Confederate general. Soon, the name was shortened to "Beau." But as the workers got to know him more, and like him more, they honored him with the blacker moniker: "Beaudango." Which everyone shortened to "Dango" and that's what all of us at school began to call him.

In 1961 Cleveland was a black city. Once you left the Heights and headed for the city center, you passed through a section of town for about 100 blocks, where black Cleveland lived. Thousands of homes on numbered streets stretched for miles on either side of the main arteries of Carnegie and Euclid Avenues, before you reached the downtown office buildings and stores. No one in those days called it a ghetto or slum, it was just black. It was an area you never went to, if you were a boy from Roxboro Junior High and US – which is how most everyone in Cleveland referred to University School.

Funny thing was, except for the Cleveland Symphony Orchestra (one of the two or three best in the country), white Cleveland had no personality. It was known for nothing – except for being the butt of jokes. Hell, Bob Hope came from Cleveland, even owned part of the Cleveland Indians for a while, and still made jokes about the city. So, for entertainment, white teenagers in the Heights had to make do with school dances, weekend movies, or, if you were lucky, a party at a country club. No wonder we drank beer and no wonder we looked to black Cleveland for excitement. They were having fun!

Almost the only music you ever heard coming out of the Star Chief's AM radio was from Cleveland's best black station – WJMO. Their DJs labeled it: "The black spot on your dial!" No *How Much Is That Doggie In The Window?* or *Purple People Eater*, or other bubble-gum nonsense, would interrupt a steady stream of Ike and Tina,

The Coasters, B.B. King, The Temptations, The Shirelles and other great black singers.

In fact, the beginning of that July evening began when Dango called to tell me The Coasters were appearing at a black club near downtown. It was a club called Gleason's and we'd gone there once before with Jerome to hear B.B. King. We'd loved it and the clientele had loved having us there. Two other US students and their dates joined Dango, myself and our dates. Jerome would meet us down there with his date. The girls the US boys brought were all from one or the other of Cleveland's two all-girl prep schools – Hathaway Brown and Laurel. No one in our group was older than 18 or younger than 16, and believe me, no one told their parents where they were going.

Dango and I called our dates "the two Susies" – Susie Kane and Susie Mason; both went to Laurel. Susie Kane was Jewish and dark-haired, Susie Mason Episcopalian and blonde. As if that weren't enough to tell them apart, Dango put it a baser way: "Kane has big eyes. Mason has big tits." The great thing about them was that they could laugh with us at that description. They were more friends than dates or "girlfriends." They liked to have fun, dance and drink a little beer. They might make out with us a bit when we took them home, but they were definitely off limits as far as real sex was concerned. Social boundaries prevailed in the Heights along with all the other boundaries. When Cleveland prep school guys dated prep school girls, it was understood that everybody was proceeding on to college. You could get serious, but why? Why take a chance on ruining college and that wonderful upper-middle class suburban life to follow? When a preppie got a preppie pregnant that was a scandal. It only happened to one couple my entire time in high school and the unfortunate pair had to drop out of their schools and marry. No one ever saw or heard from them again.

University School boys had to do their hunting in local public schools if they were looking for sex. Not that there was a lot of it. I'd guess half the 1961 graduating class of US were still virgins on commencement day. I'd been lucky a couple of times, working hard and talking fast with some public school girls. Dango often went with some of his warehouse friends to a black whorehouse in East Cleveland. He swore by it. I was too scared to ever join him.

Truth was there was nothing to fear in black Cleveland. If you loved their music, appreciated their women and treated them with respect, and if you had money to spend, you were welcomed and protected. Gleason's, where we went that night, was the perfect example. We arrived about 9:30, paid a $5 per-person cover charge and stayed until The Coasters had finished their last set at midnight. One of the guys had a fake ID he showed at the door and we were never asked for ID again. We were seated at a large booth to the right of the small stage and facing the dance floor. I wish I had a color photo of the scene that evening. Our booth would have popped right out. We were the only white faces in that whole big, crowded room, and yet we belonged. We drank, we ate (I forget what), we laughed and we danced and danced some more. Black guys came up and asked politely to dance with our dates; we said it was up to the girls, and they accepted with pleasure, mainly because prep school boys made lousy dance partners. Even a couple of The Coasters, on their break, asked the two Susies to dance. I could just hear the Susies telling that story back at Laurel next semester. It was all that open. It was all that much fun.

After the last set, Jerome walked with our group to our cars. The rain had just ended. The downtown streets were shiny.

"See you Monday, Dango," he said, as he waved goodbye. "Take it easy back to the Heights. Only cops out this late."

That was the second time I heard the nickname that would stick for the rest of his life. I heeded Jerome's warning taking the girls home. They sat close to us, heads on our shoulders, tired out from all the dancing. I wondered if they knew just how special a night it had been. When we dropped them off there was no making out, only a walk to the door and a friendly kiss. The night had been exhilarating enough for all of us as it was.

"God, I wish I could dance," Dango said later, as we sat with the top down in the Pontiac back on North Park.

"Hey, at least you tried," I answered. "You were the only one to dance with one of the black chicks."

"Was she hot or what?!"

"She was hot. And she danced your ass off!"

He finished the last of his Schafer's.

"Okay, let's take me home," Dango said. "Hopefully I can get in without waking the bitch."

He was talking about his mother; they were that close. I started the Star Chief, pulled back onto North Park heading west, the dark ravine on our left, Roxboro Junior High on our right. I was driving toward Delaware, Dango's street, on the other side of the school athletic fields. When I got there, I cut the engine and we coasted downhill on Delaware to Dango's house. He vaulted over the passenger door so as not to make any noise.

"Call me tomorrow," he whispered and then walked up his driveway to the back door.

I kept coasting down to Cedar Boulevard, re-started the car and headed back up to my home. I smiled remembering all the good times at Gleason's. I shook my head, knowing that the newly-named Dango and his mother would never get along. And then I woke up.

I was never going to be driving to my home again in the Star Chief. I was sitting in the goddamned aisle seat of a Greyhound bus headed for Las Vegas. Boy, did I know how to screw up a summer. I glanced over at Dango; he was in the window seat staring vacantly out at the cars passing us. So I decided to look around the bus interior. There were only a few empty seats. Sunday must have been a good day to go to Vegas. Seemed to me the passengers made up a representative cross-section of California, definitely not the Heights. Quite a few older couples – white, black, and an Asian pair who kept laughing and practicing for riches to come with one of those small hand-held one-arm bandits. There were a couple of soldiers in uniform, not seated together. A Mexican family – Mom, Dad and two kids, had the back row of seats. Then there were a couple of guys that looked like they'd scraped their last few bucks off skid row and hadn't showered for a week. The bus didn't stink, but it didn't surprise me when Dango opened our window as far as it would go.

"No way I can do this all the way back to Cleveland," he said.

"What's the alternative?" I answered.

"We win enough in Vegas to fly. Or . . ."

He left the "or" hanging there and, of course, I bit.

"Or what?"

"We hitchhike."

"Hitchhike!" I said.

That was the first mention Dango had made about the two of us sticking out our thumbs to try and cross 2,500 miles of the continent, He must have thought about it before. I can assure you, I never had. Upper-middle class boys from Cleveland Heights did not hitchhike. We didn't know anyone who hitchhiked. I, however, knew Dango well enough to know this was a serious proposal. And I knew it was thrown out there as a challenge to his always careful and cautious best friend. He didn't say it, but I heard it: "You got the balls, Lee?"

I pulled the lever on the side of my seat, put it back as far as it would go, then closed my eyes and actually began to consider it. It would certainly show my father and brother a thing or two. After the Greyhound took five hours to get to Las Vegas, with stops in Pomona, San Bernardino, Barstow and Baker, hitchhiking almost made sense.

In 1961, Las Vegas was tiny; there couldn't have been more than

100,000 people who actually lived there. The Greyhound depot was a few blocks away from the downtown casinos. The second you stepped off the bus someone was handing you small flyers promising free drinks, $2 dinners, the most generous slots or naked dancing girls.

Dango and I had two bags each, small over-the-shoulder duffels and large nondescript, ubiquitous Samsonite suitcases – his black, mine gray. I waited by the side of the bus for the driver to open the luggage bay and set the bags on the sidewalk while Dango ran into the station to take a quick leak. Dango's was one of the first bags out. I watched the driver start to lift it with one hand and then switch to two. He grunted getting it to the curb. I went to pick it up to pass it back to Dango, who had just reappeared, and I couldn't lift it with one arm. It must have weighed 90 pounds. I looked at Dango.

"Weights," he said.

"You brought your weights?!"

I had completely forgotten about the set of 25 lb dumbbells that Dango had carted all the way from Cleveland. He did curls every morning at Sequoia before taking his shower. I guess I thought he had left them with the Pontiac. I don't know to this day what weights cost, but I know they're not much and the ones Dango had in his suitcase sure weren't gold plated. Didn't make any difference to him. He brought them. He was taking them back. He reached down picked up the suitcase with one hand, threw his duffel over the other shoulder and started walking down the street.

"Come on," he said. "Let's find a motel."

"Right behind you," I replied, as I picked up my bags.

We'd seen a couple of motels near the bus station when we'd pulled in and they looked to be in our price range. To 18-year-olds, Las Vegas seemed like a grown-up amusement park. Of course, that's exactly what it was, but in 1961 there was nothing like it anywhere else in the country. You'd be driving along through a not-particularly-scenic desert, go over a rise and suddenly there was more glitz and tastelessness than a teenager could ever desire. All the casinos in downtown faced the street and all doors were open. The slots were one step inside the open doors; you could sit on a stool inside the casino, play the one-armed bandit and still have one foot on the sidewalk. The slots took coins only: pennies, nickels, dimes, quarters, halves, and silver dollars. Chips were only for blackjack and table games. Even in the middle of summer, when it was hotter than the San Joaquin, the doors were wide open and the air-conditioning was cranked-up. You'd walk by on the sidewalk and get hit by a cool breeze. Waitresses in skimpy tutus and too much make-up would wander around the slot machines passing out free drinks. Dango and I sauntered slowly down the main drag, darting in occasionally to play a quarter slot, trying to look like what we thought a 21-year-old would look like, trying to figure out which casino would be the least likely to question our age.

We both had driver's licenses from the state of Maine that proved we were 21. In fact, quite a few of our classmates at US had bogus Maine licenses. I don't remember who discovered it in our class, but Maine made it easy for us to get pretty legit-looking IDs. You sent a letter to the Maine Department of Motor Vehicles informing them that you would be moving to Maine in the next few months. They would send you a blank application form to be typed in with all your pertinent data. Then when you came to Maine and passed the driver's test, they would emboss a portion of the form with the State Seal and that would be your driver's license. No photo required. Perfect for enterprising high school students from Ohio who had no intention of ever setting foot in Maine. We simply filled out the forms with our new birth dates, had a girl with good handwriting fake the Maine Secretary of State's signature and then double emboss each license with Dango's mom's notary seal. That simple. If somebody really wanted to challenge your ID, you simply walked away. But most places wanted your business. Las Vegas casinos were like most places.

Dango and I had our gambling plan all set. It was mutually agreed I was the best gambler. I had taken some big pots from some of our richer friends at US. We would both try our luck for a little while with the one armed bandits. You never know, one of us might hit a big jackpot. The main effort though, would be me at the blackjack tables. We were no fools. We knew the odds of winning at blackjack were a lot better than winning on the slots.

Before gambling, we fortified ourselves with a $2, all-you-can-eat, prime rib dinner at the Golden Horseshoe. When we finished, which took a while (Dango went back for three helpings), we quietly edged into the casino, got a bucket of quarters and hit the one- armed bandits. After about 10 minutes, I was up about $20 and I suddenly hit a $100 jackpot on a quarter machine. I thought I'd robbed a bank. Bells started going off, the quarters came flying out in the trough and on the floor, and some little totem pole light on top of the bandit kept flashing. Eventually a change girl came over, put a key in the machine to cut the clamor and helped me with my winnings. A small crowd gathered around to congratulate me. I kept waiting for a tap on the shoulder from some casino executive to ask my age, but it never came. Must have looked pretty funny 'cause I could see Dango laughing his ass off just behind my well-wishers. The next thing I knew, I was the proud recipient of eleven $10 Golden Horseshoe chips, two crisp $20 bills, five silver dollars and three quarters. We were well on our way to flying back to Cleveland and I was on my way to the blackjack tables.

Most of the tables were $1 minimum. There were some for big spenders with $5 minimum and even a few where you could start with quarters. I watched the $1 tables to spot the dealer who seemed to be having the worst luck. I found a cute woman dealer who laughed and joked with her players and didn't seem to win all that much. I decided to start with her, cashed in two of my $10 chips for silver dollars and began to play. She hit two blackjacks right after I sat down and I lost my first five hands. Then a tall Asian dealer, who dealt like a robot, only talked to players to call cards and payoffs and never changed his flat expression, relieved her. He turned out to be my man. For a run of about 16 hands he was always between 12 and 16, would take a hit, and bust. Betting aggressively, doubling down when I could and not taking any risky hits, I quickly jumped up another $100. When they switched dealers again, I decided to take my winnings and run.

If you added my new $230 to the $500 Dango and I left Los Angeles with, that was a fortune in 1961. I figured it was plenty for two one-way airline tickets back to Cleveland. Giddy with pride and excitement at my gambling prowess, I grabbed Dango by the slots and we exited the Horseshoe into the warm Las Vegas night.

"How'd you do?" I asked.

"Not great. I dropped about $45," Dango answered.

"How can you lose $45 on quarter slots?"

"I don't know. I played some half dollar and dollar machines, too."

"Well I'm up a little over 200. We should go check some airfares."

"Whoa, that's fantastic. We'll start checking flights tomorrow. I got a better idea."

"What?" I asked, ready to pour cold water on just about anything.

"Lido de Paris at the Stardust. Beautiful naked women."

"Bob, it's going to cost money." With serious stuff, I always reverted to his real name.

"Nah, we've got plenty. It's only five bucks each for the show. The night is young. Are we going to go sit in that lousy motel room and watch TV? When will you ever be in Vegas again?"

I was supposed to be the sensible one, but we're talking about a sensible 18-year-old male trying to resist the call of "beautiful naked women." He was right about the motel room, too. What possessed us to stay near the Greyhound station, I'll never know. I think we could have gotten a better room at the Golden Horseshoe for about the same $12-a-night price. Next thing I knew, Dango moved in to close the sale.

"Lee, how hard was it winning over 200 bucks? Do you know it took you less than an hour?"

"You never know about cards," I warned.

That was the last word of caution for the night, because Dango wasn't even listening to me. He was hailing a cab he saw on the street. In less than a minute, we were leaving downtown Las Vegas heading out to an area they called "the Strip."

In 1961, all of the Strip was out of town to the west on the main highway headed to Los Angeles. All the famous Vegas hotels were there. I think the Flamingo was the furthest out of town, and then the Tropicana, Sands, Wilbur Clark's Desert Inn, Riviera, Sahara and closest to town, The Stardust. I wouldn't swear to their locations, but I can tell you all I thought they were when we passed them on the way into town – glorified motels with big, fancy illuminated signs out front and casinos attached. The Desert Inn looked like the only one with buildings that wouldn't blow away in a heavy sandstorm. The Stardust probably had the longest, gaudiest sign, but that was to cover up the cheapest looking motel rooms behind it.

It didn't take long to reach The Stardust, or cost much either – only $4.50. Dango generously tossed the cabbie a five. I was along for the ride now. I knew it would do no good to point out to him that was just another five I'd have to win back tomorrow. He must have been checking show times, because we were right on time for the evening's first performance. We paid the $5 cover, got our tickets and proceeded to the show entrance. Dango handed the tickets to the maître d', or whatever the hell you call the guy who seats you at a Vegas show, he looked us over and started heading up and away from the stage. Then Dango did something I never expected; he grabbed the guy by the arm, whispered something in his ear while pointing to a small empty table closer to the stage and slipped him a $20. Our usher nodded, took us to the table and said he hoped we'd enjoy the show.

"Where'd you ever learn to do that?" I asked once we were seated.

"I don't know. Saw it in a movie. You didn't want to sit way up there, did you?"

"No, these seats are great, but we've blown $30 already."

"Lee, in 20 years . . ."

"Okay, I got it."

And I did get it; Dango just got it a lot more naturally than I did. I knew we were doing something we would probably never do again, so let go and let it happen. I decided to sit back and enjoy the show. Then I saw the little tent card on the table that informed me there was a three-drink minimum per person. After that, I just began to laugh.

The laughter kept going right through the Lido de Paris. Even Dango had to laugh. I have no idea if the Lido in Paris is better, or sexier, or what, but after the experience at The Stardust, I swore I'd never pay a penny to find out. As for "beautiful naked women" it should have read "beautiful naked female breasts". The showgirls came out dressed in skimpy outfits covered with thousands of sequins that glittered in the lights. They didn't dance much. They sort of pranced from place to place and posed. I guess they were all "beautiful" but we were sitting close enough to see all the make-up caked on their faces. They could have had beards under the make-up for all we knew. They looked statuesque; their outfits were so tight their breasts thrust out like they were on stage. They were: the half-cups for the breasts held them out and up for inspection. They didn't move much. In fact, I don't think they moved at all and they sure as hell weren't sexy. The only thing that came close to sexy in the show was one dancer who appeared "naked" accompanied by six giant white feathers. She proceeded to tease the audience by dancing and manipulating those feathers so skillfully that you never saw anything. By that time, Dango and I had finished our three $5 beers and left. Outside, feeling no pain, still laughing, we decided to walk back to our motel.

"Do you remember Blaze Starr at the Roxy?" I asked.

"How could I ever forget Blaze?" Dango replied.

"Well, the Lido de Paris definitely needs Blaze."

That was all it took to get Dango and I reminiscing about that cold Friday night back in Cleveland when we'd gone downtown to the Roxy Theater to see the famous stripper Blaze Starr.

We had actually been to the Roxy a couple of times in our Junior Year, before making this February trip. It was a tawdry, little burlesque house on a side street just a block or so away from Public Square, the hub of downtown Cleveland. The Roxy was Cleveland's only, and last, burlesque theater. I don't think there's one left in the whole country now. They've been replaced with strip clubs and massage parlors as our culture's progressed. Back in the '20s or '30s the Roxy might have been a small, legit theater, but you had to go through back alleys and turn dark corners to find it in the '60s. Larger, fancier theaters that showed first run movies were over on Euclid Avenue just off the square.

That night there were four of us from US: Dango, myself and two other classmates. We split in two pairs after we parked the Pontiac so we would avoid entering the Roxy looking like exactly what we were – a group of teenage boys. We let the other two go first and once they got in, we waited a minute or so, then went up to the window and each paid our $7.50. The Roxy was more expensive than the Lido in Vegas, but they didn't serve drinks. The interior of the theater was a wreck. Every row seemed to have one or two broken seats. Lights along the wall were out. There was a small balcony section, but it was always dark and I never saw anyone in it the few times I was there. I would guess full capacity at about 150, but the Blaze Starr night was the most crowded I had ever seen it, and there were no more than 60 men. The majority of those "men" were boys like us, except a little older, already in college, already feeling no pain from whatever they had been drinking. The rest of the audience consisted of blue collar guys in baseball caps, a couple of business men in suits and, in three or four single-seats in the back or by the walls, wherever it was darkest, strange seedy men sat with overcoats and hats on their laps.

The theater went completely dark, the curtain went up, lights illuminated the bare stage and the show began. Not with Blaze, of course, she was the headliner, but with bad comedians, mediocre jugglers and acrobats, and a very pathetic magician. I can't imagine where they got the money to pay these supporting bit players. I can't imagine, with the size of the audience, where they got the money to pay anybody, but there it was and it was awful. The four of us from US joined with the college kids blurting out catcalls and derisive comments aimed at the comics. Didn't stop them, just encouraged them and they'd fire back at the audience with dirtier remarks. Two strippers were interspersed between the bad comedy and other performers, but I don't recall a thing about them.

On the marquee outside the Roxy and on her picture poster in the lobby the headline read, "Blaze Starr and Her Twin 44s!" She was depicted wearing a cowboy hat on her head and a rawhide vest covering the hardware and nothing else. Burlesque in the '60s promised a lot, but only went so far. Total nudity was not allowed. Girls were always supposed to keep their G-strings on and their nipples covered with a pasty of some kind. Blaze was known for bending the rules a little. When the curtain went up and Blaze emerged, the small crowd went crazy. The outfit she had on was pure Dale Evans: the cowboy hat, rawhide vest, sequined Western shirt, full-length rawhide skirt, double holsters with six-guns and studded cowboy boots. Any other resemblance to Roy's wife ended when the music began and Blaze started taking off the outfit.

Unlike the "beautiful naked women" of the Lido de Paris, Blaze moved. Every part of Blaze moved. She was not a tall woman, but she was big in all the right places and she loved showing those places. If I'd known the adjective then, I'd have called her "Rubenesque." She hit all the downbeats at just the right time with the removal of another piece of clothing, or the revealing of another piece of flesh. She had fun while she did it, teasing the audience and taunting them with every article of clothing she removed. All the college and high school boys were cheering her on to take it off.

When she finally got down to her G-string and tasseled pasties, the music paused, and then started again for her "naked" dance. She proceeded to bump and grind to the music for five more minutes. Most of the audience was standing, whistling and shouting. I guess it was sexy, but in almost a wholesome, fun kind of way. Like you were watching some voluptuous female sex goddess, whom you could never touch, but who would spark your imagination to new heights of lustful male fantasies. Dango elbowed me during this final dance and gestured to a man sitting at the end of our aisle. He was one of the sad, little men in the dark with hat and overcoat in his lap. He was still seated, his eyes glued on Blaze, his hands hard at work under his coat and our whole row was shaking. Dango and I looked at each other, shook our heads and laughed, then looked back to Blaze for her finale.

Now I swear I remember this, but I still can't believe it: Blaze strode to the center of the stage, spread her legs slightly and grabbed each of those "twin 44s" in her hands. Then she proceeded to twirl those cannons and attached tassels in opposite directions! She took her hands off, placed them on her knees and thrust the star performers forward at the audience. All the while spinning them, one clockwise, one counter-clockwise. When the music reached its peak, she grabbed a tassel in each hand, ripped them off and threw them to the frenzied audience. Then she stood proudly, in only G-string and giant bare breasts, as the curtain quickly dropped. Don't let anyone ever tell you there weren't real stars in burlesque.

As we approached our seedy motel in downtown Vegas, Dango and I did a price comparison: $15 for two to see Blaze versus $40 plus tip for two at the Lido de Paris. Why had we wasted our money? Now I had to go back to the blackjack tables the next day to win at least a couple of hundred more to get back on a flight.

At the entrance to our motel three guys were talking, smoking and passing around a quart bottle of cheap beer. I was talking to Dango and didn't pay them any mind as we walked up to turn in the driveway and head to our room. Suddenly one of the guys grabbed hold of my arm and drunkenly began shouting close to my face, "Hey man, hey, you gotta help us, help us out with a few bucks so we can get something to eat."

Before I could pull my arm away or even respond, Dango picked him up, ripped him off me and threw him on the driveway. Then he clinched his fist and started toward him on the ground, not shouting, but growling his words, "You want something to eat? I'll give you something to eat."

He reached down with his one arm, grabbed my stunned assailant by the collar and drew back his other hand in a fist. The other two guys had already run off, when I got to Dango and stayed his arm.

"Dango, Dango, it's okay. He's just drunk. Let him go."

Dango released his collar and in an instant the drunk was up and chasing after his friends. I kept holding on to Dango, because I'd seen him lose his temper before and knew what he could do when angered.

"I'll kill that fucker!" he said, still growling. "What's he think he's doing, grabbing people? He could've had a knife, Lee."

"I know, I know, but it's over now. He almost died of fright anyway. Look, he pissed himself," I said, releasing him and pointing to a small wet spot on the pavement.

Dango looked down and laughed. Just as quickly as the fury had come, it was gone. We continued up the driveway to our room.

"I scared the piss out of him, didn't I?"

"You scared the piss out of me too." I answered. "Let's get to the room so I can empty it."

We woke up late Monday morning and did a re-assessment of our finances. I still had the $250 I left LA with, plus about $220 from winnings, but I'd paid for the Lido de Paris and the $2 dinners, so that took off a good $45. That left me with about $415. Dango had lost $90, tipped the guy at the Lido $20, paid for the cab and other miscellaneous stuff so he was left with about $125 from his original $250. Since we planned on spending one more day in Vegas the motel would cost a little over $50. We'd have to eat, so that would be another $25. Totaling it up, we were at about $465 – down $35 since we left LA, not up.

"Well, you just have to win $100 more than yesterday," Dango said. "And you've got a full day to do it. Only took you a couple of hours to win $200."

"No sweat," I replied facetiously. Dango really didn't know anything about playing cards.

We went back to the Golden Horseshoe for breakfast and somehow ended up paying more for it than an all-you-can-eat prime rib dinner. After that, I took my time and started to look for a down-on-his-luck dealer. No one at the Horseshoe caught my eye, so we went down the street to the Four Queens. I spotted another Asian dealer at a $1 table and decided to give it a try. Maybe I thought Asian dealers were lucky for me. I was about to find out about luck.

In less than 20 minutes I was down $135. I think I'd won only one hand and I was beginning to panic. I decided to go for a big bet and put out a $10 chip. I got a pair of tens and the dealer was showing a four of clubs. Easy call. I doubled down, doubling my bet. I hit a jack on one ten and a nine on the other. I was sitting pretty. The dealer flipped his hole card – it was a deuce. Then he hit himself quickly and called each card and his running total as he flipped them out.

"Tres – nine, a five – fourteen, seven, twenty-one."

Twenty more dollars gone in one hand. I decided to take a break for a while, lick my wounds and count my money. I had set $300 as my betting limit, which left me about $150 to recoup my losses. But I had lost my luck and any semblance of confidence I might have had. I was also beginning to form a theory about gambling, which I still believe to this day – when you have to win, you lose.

Dango saw me get up from the table and came over to me, "Not good, huh?"

"Bad. My luck's gone."

"Why don't we take $150 and put it on red in roulette?" Dango suggested.

"You'd do that?" I countered.

"Why not? It's better than watching a slow death with you at blackjack."

"I thought I was dying pretty quick."

We were walking through the casino and what should appear – the only roulette table working that morning. I handed Dango my last ten $10 chips and my last ten $5 chips.

"Go for it. My luck's shot."

He didn't even hesitate. In a second all the chips were on red and the wheel was spinning.

"Sixteen red," the croupier announced.

"Alright, Dango, get it off of there and let's go," I shouted.

He made no move to pick it up.

"One more spin and we're on a plane out of here. I feel lucky." He let it ride.

"Twenty-nine black."

"Whoops," Dango said, looking at me with a smile. "Easy come, easy go."

Funny thing, I wasn't upset either. I was relieved.

"Let's go," I said.

"Go where?"

"Back to our room."

"Why?"

"So we can start figuring how this hitchhiking is going to work."

We went back. I got a USA road map from an ESSO station near the motel and we started to plot a course that seemed reasonable back to Cleveland. What we'd soon discover is that you can't figure anything out ahead of time when it comes to hitchhiking.

CHAPTER 3

Las Vegas to Seligman

Tuesday morning, August 8, 1961, we began our hitchhiking careers. Neither of us had ever hitchhiked before, but how hard could it be? It was a typical Las Vegas August morning, no clouds, 85 degrees at 9:00 a.m. The motel owner gave us two large sheets of white paper, a black magic marker and some masking tape. After we paid the bill, of course. I wrote "STUDENTS" in big letters on one sheet, "OHIO" on the other and then taped one to Dango's Samsonite and one to mine.

The owner also told us which road we had to take to head south and hit the famed Route 66, the main highway between Los Angeles and Chicago. It was a street on the east edge of Las Vegas called Boulder Highway. It crossed the Colorado River at Lake Mead going over Boulder Dam and then passing through about 100 miles of desert until it hooked up with Route 66 at Kingman, Arizona. We'd plotted that all out on our map the night before, and I have to admit, I was as anxious and excited to get going as Dango.

With the motel bill paid, we had almost exactly $75 apiece left from the $500 we left LA with. Right off the bat, we had another unexpected expense – the only way to get to Boulder Highway with our bags was by taxi, another $10.

In 1961, Boulder Highway marked Las Vegas' eastern boundary. It was a straight two-lane highway bordered on either side by lots of sagebrush, a few cheap motels, small mini/market liquor stores, Mexican restaurants, gas stations and automobile junkyards. We had the cabbie drop us by one of the market/liquor stores with a large dusty parking area in front facing the highway. We took turns going into the market to get breakfasts of orange juice, coffee and Snickers bars. At 9:35 a.m., I faced the suitcases so the signs could be read by the on-coming southbound traffic and Dango put out his thumb. I knew the time exactly, because I checked my watch.

By 10:50 a.m. we hadn't budged. Not a car had stopped. I was no longer anxious and excited.

"What makes you think we can do this all the way to Cleveland," I snapped at Dango.

"Don't go negative," he replied. "C'mon, make it fun. See that sign on the phone pole. Bet you I'll get us a ride before you hit the sign with one of those stones."

He pointed to the gravel that was all around us. I decided to play along, because there wasn't anything else to do.

"What do I win if I hit the sign before you get a ride?"

"I don't know, a buck?"

This was the first of hundreds of hitchhiking games we played to pass the waiting time. We never paid each other a penny. After about 15 cars had passed, I hit the sign and we swapped jobs.

"You owe me a buck," I said, as I stuck out my thumb.

Just as I did, a turquoise 1958 Plymouth Belvedere convertible, top down, pulled over with a guy and a girl that looked about our age.

"Hey, hop in the back," the Plymouth driver said, as his girl opened the passenger door and raised the passenger seat for us to get in. Dango and I didn't need to be told twice. We put our bags next to us on the back seat and flopped in before they could change their minds. I'd gotten us our first ride. We were on our way.

"Are you going far?" Dango asked.

"Are you guys crazy?" the driver said, ignoring him. "Are you really going to Ohio?"

"Yup, Cleveland," Dango answered.

The girl, who was quite cute, looked over the front seat at us. "Didn't anyone ever tell you? No one hitchhikes in Las Vegas."

"Why is that?"

"People lose all their money here," she said. "They get desperate, then they hitchhike and rob and kill people."

"Really!" Dango and I said at the same moment.

The driver laughed and then added his two cents, "No, probably not. But that's what people in Vegas think, so they never pick up hitchhikers."

"How come you picked us up?" Dango asked.

"I passed you guys about a half-hour ago when I went to pick up Jenny. I figured if you were still there when I came back, I'd help you out."

"Thanks," I said. "So I guess that means you're not heading to Arizona."

"No." He laughed again. "I live out this way, so I'm going to drop you by a little casino up here. At least the traffic you get there will all be heading out of town."

"Thanks for the help," I said.

"Hey, you're young, you're nuts. Gotta support the spirit."

A little strange philosophy for our first ride, but not a bad start. They dropped us by a small bar casino that had a sign out front: "Last Chance to Gamble." We set our bags up under the sign and stuck our thumbs out again.

Next ride took us a couple of miles or so into the small town of

Boulder City, Nevada. The town was created to house the workers who built the dam back in the '30s and '40s. There was one stoplight in the town where the highway turned to head toward Boulder Dam and Arizona. That was our next hitching spot. It was already about 1:30 in the afternoon, the temperature must have been 110 degrees and the traffic was pretty light. We took turns hitching and sitting in the shade of a small store by the road. After almost an hour, a small cube delivery truck pulled over and stopped. Dango ran over to the cab.

"You really going to Ohio?" the driver asked.

"Yes sir," Dango answered. "Cleveland."

"Okay, throw your stuff in back and ride up with me. I'll get you to Kingman."

He got out to open up the back of the truck. Dango and I looked at each other with big grins, placed our bags on the wooden floor bed next to a load of stacked cardboard boxes, then climbed in the cab next to him to begin our first long ride.

"Been a long time since I've picked up any riders, but the Ohio sign got me," the driver said. "Then when you said 'Yes sir' I was definitely going to pick you up. I used to be a Marine."

The signs worked. Letting drivers know you had a specific destination to go to gave them a sense of comfort. Politeness helped, too. Once you made people feel at ease, most of them wanted to give you a lift. Driving long stretches of road by yourself is lonely. Picking up two clean-cut students on their way to Ohio, what could be the harm? Dango and I were getting the hang of it: we projected the innocence of choirboys.

Our driver was half-owner of four Texaco stations, three in Vegas and one in Kingman. He had to make the Vegas-Kingman run every week to keep the Arizona station stocked with auto parts, gum and candy. He was a good guy and pointed out places of interest along the highway. He stopped a few minutes at Boulder Dam so that Dango and I could get out, look down its sheer face and feel the enormity of the achievement. When we got back in the truck, I grabbed the window seat and let Dango take the middle. Everything seemed new with hitchhiking. Because I wasn't driving the way I did on the trip out, I could actually look at the country we were passing through. On this leg, I saw quite a few Indians, Hopi I guess, selling 'authentic Indian jewelry' in small roadside stands, driving beat-up, paint-worn pick-up trucks or gathered around dilapidated trailer homes in the middle of nowhere. That was about it except for what seemed like thousands of miles of empty desert punctuated every few miles or so with jagged buttes and rugged, barren small mountains. It didn't look like anything could live out there, and then you'd see three or four vultures circling something off to the side of the road and you'd flash back to your high school biology class and realize there was an entire eco-system out there fighting their own Darwinian battles. On the drive from Cleveland to Sequoia, I'd never seen any of it, never thought about it.

We pulled into the Texaco station in Kingman, Arizona about 3:15, except when we'd entered Arizona there had been a time change, so it was now 4:15 p.m. Our ex-Marine gave us a couple of candy bars and two ice-cold Cokes from the station for energy. Then, he pointed to the highway running in front of the station.

"That's Route 66, boys. Stay on it headed east, you'll be in Ohio in no time."

He said the last words with a chuckle and then shook our hands.

"Good luck," he said, and hopped back in his truck and drove it behind the station.

Dango and I picked up our bags, headed up to the highway and put our thumbs out once more. As far as we could tell we were sort of in the center of town, so we decided to walk along the road headed east and see if we could find a better place to hitch. We walked on the side shoulder, backs to the traffic, bags in our right hands, thumbs out and up on our left hands. We couldn't have walked more than 100 yards when a Highway Patrol car pulled in front of us and stopped. A big Highway Patrol Officer got out and stood by the driver door facing us.

"Great," I thought to myself. "All we need is to get arrested in Kingman, Arizona. I'll have to call my dad from jail."

In the Heights, I'd been pulled over by cops a few times. I'd gotten one speeding ticket and a couple of warnings. But that was the Heights; cops tended to cut the kids of residents a little slack. Especially white kids from "good families." The Highway Patrol had another reputation altogether. They were known to be hard asses. All you needed to do was watch Broderick Crawford on the TV series. They dealt with real criminals. They shot guys. On the drive out, Dango and I had kept a sharp lookout for patrol cars, and when we spotted them, we made sure to be right on or below the speed limit. Spotting them was relatively easy in 1961, too. I had never heard of, or seen, an unmarked patrol car. They all had black and white paint jobs and flashing lights on top. Sometimes now, when I'm driving in traffic, I wonder how Dango and I got away with open beers in the car, breaking speed limits and just plain reckless driving. Luck, obviously, played a part, but I keep coming back to one thing – there were fewer cars on the road. Fewer drivers. Fewer police. And, outside of the cities, especially when you were crossing the middle of the country, the highways were "the wide open spaces."

"Are we not allowed to hitch here, sir?" Dango asked so politely as he walked up to the imposing patrolman.

"No, you're fine. 66 is an open access highway. You can hitch almost anywhere. It's just not very safe along this stretch. Someone tries to stop here, they could cause an accident. Jump in the back. I'll take you up the road a way where it's better."

We got in the back with our bags and when he closed the door it automatically locked. We were in the "cage" and I thought for a minute it was an easy way for him to take us in. But no, he was being a nice guy and shortly dropped us off by a drive-in restaurant where there was plenty of room to pull off. So much for mean, tough Brodrick Crawford and his Highway Patrol series. I kept expecting harassment from cops during our trip and it never happened, even when it should have.

Dango started setting up the bags. I went into the restaurant to take the first pee break. There were a couple of pay-phones by the door and, since I hadn't talked to the parents after leaving Los Angeles, I thought it was time. I figured the time in Cleveland to be about 7:30 p.m. and, because my dad often worked late, I had a good chance of talking to my mom. I put in a dime, which I immediately got back when I placed a collect call.

My mom answered, accepted the charges, and started with a question: "Where are you honey?"

"Kingman, Arizona."

"Arizona? I thought you'd be a lot closer than that."

"That's why I called. Dango and I spent a couple of days in Vegas. Just got on the road again today."

Now you'll notice this was not a complete lie. We were on the road again, just not in a Greyhound bus.

"Oh, Lee . . . Are you guys okay? Do you need money?"

See, this was why I wanted to get my mom. My dad at this point would have blown his top and asked more probing questions. Mom was just relieved that we were alright.

"No, we're fine. It's very slow-going, that's all. Probably be about three days 'til we're home. Stops everywhere. Oh, Mom we're pulling out. Gotta run."

"Okay, hon. Call again when you're closer, so I don't worry."

"I will, Mom. Say 'hi' to Dad. Don't worry. Bye."

I hung up, feeling proud of myself for buying time, not really lying and not really telling the truth. Teenagers never change.

Cars and trucks cruising along Route 66 definitely had places to go and things to do. There weren't many of them looking to pick up hitchhikers. A lot of the cars were packed with family vacationers: never a good bet to stop for a stranger. For large semis, it was too much of a hassle to pull off, down shift and stop. Two hours must have passed before a small pick-up truck with a single guy pulled over and we got back on the road again. The sun was low in the sky behind us as we headed east for our first long ride on 66.

Our new driver appeared to be about 45 with dark hair and a two-day stubble. He didn't talk much, which might have been the reason I thought he was part Indian. After we got out of Kingman, he said the only thing I remember from the ride: "I'm heading to Prescott. Turn off's about 100 miles up here after Seligman. I'll drop you there."

Two hours later, Dango and I were standing, under a streetlight, in front of a mini-market gas station in Seligman, Arizona. There were a couple of gas stations and a motel on the other side of 66, and it looked like another gas station and motel up the highway from us on our side. You couldn't see anything else because past the pools of light illuminating the businesses and the road itself, it was pitch black. I raised my head to look up at the bright light above us and saw thousands of large and small insects dancing around it. Large black moths would dart in and out of the melee of smaller insects. One of the moths swooped close by my head as I was looking up and I realized they weren't moths at all, but bats. Whoa, Dango and I had landed in the opening scene of a horror film.

We walked into the market to get some dinner and assess our situation. We got a piece of day-old chewy pizza out of a warmer and some orange juice out of the refrigeration unit (we were trying to eat "healthy"). There was an old guy behind the counter, wearing a cowboy shirt, sitting on a stool and reading Rogue, one of the trashy girlie magazines Playboy killed when it really got rolling in the '60s. He looked up when we approached the counter to pay.

"That'll be 80 cents for the juices," he said. Then without warning, he turned and spit into a spittoon behind the counter. The "ping" of the spittle hitting metal acted as an exclamation point. Dango and I both jumped.

"And," he began again, "I can't charge ya anything for the pizza. Wouldn't be fair, seein' as how I was just about to throw it out."

Dango and I looked at each other thinking the same thing: Free food!

"Thanks," we said together.

We started to head out the door and he called after us,

"You guys aren't drivin', are ya?"

"No, we're hitching." Dango said.

"To Ohio," I added.

"Good luck," he said, shaking his head and going back to his magazine.

We sat down by our bags to eat our dinner and discuss our options.

"We've got to catch an all-night ride," Dango said. "We wait under that light, drivers can see us and there's open space to pull off."

I glanced out at the highway as a semi barreled past at about 50 miles per hour. Seligman was even too small to rate a speed trap.

"Greyhound's gotta go through here. Maybe we could take it to Albuquerque?" I suggested.

"Hey, we're hitching here," Dango said. "We can't give up."

"Okay," I answered, grabbing my bag. "Let's go show our angelic faces and maybe a miracle will happen."

"Positive, Lee. Be positive," Dango said, as he got his bag and followed me out to our well-lit, insect-and-bat-infested hitching spot.

I don't think Marilyn Monroe, hiking up her skirt, could have hitched a ride out of Seligman that night. As it got later, the traffic thinned and not a soul pulled in for gas. The cars and trucks that passed seemed to go faster as it got later. Dango and I played some more of our games, but they got old quick. We were both getting tired and I was beginning to think the three-day estimated time of arrival I gave to my mother was a pipe dream. At about 11:40 p.m., the old codger who sold us the juice and gave us our free pizza came out and slowly walked over to where we were standing.

"Ya know," he said, before spitting again. "I don't think you're gonna get a ride tonight."

"Sorta looks that way," I responded, kind of hoping he was going to offer us some nice place to sleep in back of the store.

"I thought ya should know every eastbound freight has to stop in Seligman to take on water for the climb up to Flagstaff."

"Really?" Dango and I said at the same time again.

"Yup. Right behind the market's the tracks and up apiece is the water tower. Train due at midnight." With that, he turned and started walking back.

Dango and I looked at each other. This time I said it first: "In 20 years . . . ?"

CHAPTER 4

Seligman to Clovis

My bravado left me the second Dango and I walked behind the market/gas station into the darkness. As our eyes became accustomed to the moonless night, I could see that we literally were in the middle of nowhere. There were no roads, no fences, not even any trees.

In the distance, I could make out a few small houses and trailers with tall spindly TV antennas reaching as high as they could to capture whatever broadcast waves could make it to this god-forsaken place. The land seemed to be barren high desert scrub. We'd trip every fifth or sixth step on a small bush or large rock. A little to the east we could make out the water tower with some small buildings surrounding it. One of them had a light on – probably the train station – although the more I thought about it, I don't think any passenger trains would have any reason to stop there. Nearby the building was a siding of track with a couple of empty boxcars. Then we could see two lines of track running east/west right directly in front of us. We were about 175 yards from Route 66. Looking back, you could see the lights of the entire "business section" of Seligman; it looked no longer than a football field. The highway exited town at each end of the lights and, looking east or west, you could make out occasional headlights and taillights on the famous route. Traffic was almost non-existent just before midnight on a Tuesday.

"Are you sure you want to do this?" I said to Dango, now pretty sure I didn't.

"Look up," he replied, ignoring me.

I looked up and caught my breath. We were in the center of a planetarium, except it was better than a planetarium. From horizon to horizon, there were more stars than I had ever seen.

A train whistle broke the silence. We turned to the west and far down the track we saw a small light. Dango looked over at me.

"Lee, it's meant to be."

"Dango, don't give me that shit," I said. Nothing was "meant to be."

I stepped over the tracks, away from Seligman a couple of yards and threw my bags down. Then I sat down, leaned back against them and continued my stargazing. I knew one thing: two upper-middle class boys from Cleveland, hitchhiking in the middle of the Arizona desert was not high on any list of probabilities and certainly wasn't "meant to be." So we might as well continue to push the envelope and see what else would happen. I also remember thinking to myself: "Let's just see if this train stops."

Ten minutes passed and the whistle sounded again. The light didn't look all that much closer.

"How fast do you think it's going?" Dango asked.

"Maybe it's not moving."

He laughed then kicked me.

"C'mon, it's going to be fun."

Five minutes later the engines passed us going very slowly. And, sure enough, they stopped under the water tower. To the west, back down the length of the train, the cars went as far as we could see.

"Come on," Dango said, "let's go find our car."

He picked up his bags and headed down the track.

I followed, wondering how the hell we'd know which car was "ours." In the first section, most of the cars were boxcars and they were all locked on the outside by large, solid steel padlocks. There were a few low, open flat cars with various pieces of machinery bolted and strapped down with metal ties interspersed among the boxcars. We must have walked past 30 cars when Dango spotted a boxcar with its door partially open. We headed for it. Dango started to put his heavy bag in the opening, when he was startled by someone in the car offering to help. There was no telling in the dark the age or even what ethnicity the guy was, but once you got close to the car you could smell him. He started to grab Dango's bag.

"Here, I'll give you a hand."

Not expecting the weight, he almost fell out of the car. He quickly let go. Dango grabbed it back.

"That's okay," Dango said. "We'll find another car."

Dango picked up the pace and we kept heading down the train. He turned to me.

"There must have been four or five guys in there," Dango said. "Did you get a whiff of them?"

"A little," I replied. "What if that's the only open boxcar?"

"There'll be something."

But it did turn out to be the only open boxcar we came across with an open door. We could now see the end of the train and it looked like there was a caboose with a light on. We didn't want to run into any Santa Fe workers, so getting too close to the caboose was not a good idea. Dango stopped by an open car with raised sides; there were three of them in a row. He put his bags down and started to climb up the first one.

"I'm gonna look in here," he said and dropped over the edge.

I had always thought they carried coal or raw ore in cars like these, so I was pessimistic as usual. Then, a second later his head popped over the side.

"Perfect. Pass up the bags."

I couldn't back out now, although every upper-middle class bone in my body screamed that I should, so I nearly broke my back lifting Dango's Samsonite over my head to his outstretched hands. He got it, hoisted it over the side and I heard it land with a loud thud on what sounded like wood. I tossed the other bags to him and then I climbed into "our car."

We were sharing our accommodations with what appeared to me to be two giant turbines. They were bolted into the wooden floor of the car. There was enough room on either side for one person to squeeze by, and on either end, you could actually sit down and stretch out a little. If we'd had a mattress, it might even have been comfortable. Unfortunately, all we had to sit on and against were our bags, the wood flooring, and the cold steel walls of the car.

Dango promptly placed his bag flat, sat down on it and leaned back against the steel siding.

"How many miles do you think we'll cover tonight?"

"I don't know," I answered, laughing and shaking my head. "But I guess we're about to find out."

Almost as soon as I said that, the train jerked and knocked me down next to him.

"Next stop, Albuquerque." Dango said, laughing down at me as the train slowly started moving east.

Having taken a few train rides, before and since our midnight ride out of Seligman, I can tell you one thing: they all take forever. The romance of listening to the clickity-clack of the rails and enjoying the scenery pales after about two hours even if you're in a plush seat with a good book and a dining car to go to. Sitting in an open freight car with cold steel all around you, exposed to the wind and noise of the train got old in about 15 minutes. Then, to make things worse, about an hour after Seligman, the train started its climb up to Flagstaff.

Dango and I had been in T-shirts since we left Vegas. Even under the bat-infested light in Seligman at 11:00 p.m., the temperature must have been around 78 degrees. As we climbed and the wind from the train continued to hit us, the drop in temperature started reminding me of Cleveland in the winter. Dango and I didn't even have a sweater or sweatshirt between us. This was summer in the desert, for Christ's sake. We opened our bags to find anything we could put on. We both had light summer rain jackets. We put them on. We were still freezing. We each had a couple of long sleeve cotton shirts. We put those on and buttoned them up. The train kept climbing, the temperature kept dropping. Finally, we huddled together with our bags at the front end of the car, keeping low to stay out of the wind.

After a few minutes of that, I couldn't keep my teeth from chattering so I got up and began walking around the turbines, from one end of the car to the other, to try and keep warm. I could just see over the top edge of the side and now we were passing through a pine forest. What happened to the Arizona desert? I walked over to where Dango was huddled in the corner to tell him about the change in terrain only to discover that he had fallen asleep. I was tempted to wake him up, so I would not have to suffer with the cold by myself, but he looked so peaceful I decided to be a true friend. He was a big guy, even bigger wearing three shirts and a jacket, but somehow he had managed to push himself so tightly into the corner of that open rail car that he appeared no larger than a toddler curled-up in his crib. He was in the fetal position, knees tight up into his chest, elbows in, hands clasped under his chin holding his horn-rimmed glasses, his small duffel squished behind him to soften the cold steel corner. Amazing to me that he could fall asleep an hour and a half after hopping a freight train in the middle of Arizona – something I'll bet no Cleveland Heights or Shaker Heights boy had ever done.

But that was Dango. He charged through life from moment to moment, never seeming to question the things he did or fearing the consequences. He would do the extraordinary or the outrageous and somehow act as if it were commonplace. If you were his friend and accompanied him for part of the journey, it made for a great ride.

As I looked over at him completely at peace, crammed into the corner of that railroad car, I thought back to the New Year's Eve party we had attended a little over six months ago. It was at the Coolidge's, the home of one of our wealthier University School buddies, who lived in a mansion on South Park. Carleton Coolidge had talked his parents into throwing a high school New Year's party there, because the house was so large they could keep 86 drinking teenagers in the basement ballroom and rec rooms. Dango and I went together stag because, as was often the case, we were between girlfriends and the two Susies were already going with other guys.

Everyone that night seemed desperate to have fun. We were seniors and things were breaking apart. Many of the friends would not be there for the next party. These were "holding on" parties – attempts at holding on to old friends, high school and irresponsibility. Everybody drank way too much.

Dango and I arrived late after picking up another stag. We parked the Star Chief on South Park since the Coolidge's long circular driveway was already filled with cars. The year-end evening was crystal clear. It was too cold to snow. The snow had made its appearance earlier; it started falling on Christmas day and finally let up on the 30th. A good five or six feet covered the ground; the snowplows had cleared the streets and created snow banks along each roadway as high as eight feet. With streetlights, Christmas lights on all the houses and fresh clean snow, the Heights looked like a Currier and Ives Christmas card. It was beautiful to look at, not much fun to walk through. Since it was a party and we were teenagers, we wore our winter coats, but only had loafers on our feet. No boots. The walk from the street up to the Coolidge's front door was a good 200 yards over the packed snow driveway. We managed it very slowly.

We were greeted at the door by Carleton, our classmate (at least his parents hadn't named him Calvin). There were two sets of steps leading from the entry hall, one down, one up. After stomping the snow off our shoes, we were directed down. I could see a group of parents at the top of the steps going up to the first floor. I immediately thought of them as guards posted to make sure none of the partying teens broke through to the expensive Persian carpets, fine furnishings and original artworks in the main part of the house. Smart move. Down below the celebration was already in full swing.

"Where you headed?" Dango shouted at me over the din.

"I think I'll grab a beer and play a little pool for a while," I said.

Dango nodded, "I'm gonna go find Carol. No way she's leaving here tonight with Muelenberg."

Carol was a Laurel girl Dango had taken out a few times and, in my professional opinion, she didn't give a damn for Dango or our classmate, her date for the night, Muelenberg. That was the last I saw of Dango until after the New Year. Although every so often during the evening, I'd spot him somewhere in the crowd or hear him over the noise. He wasn't driving, so he was really letting go.

The stags all split up and roamed the party like wolves trying to pick up the scent of vulnerable dates. Just because we were all friends, it didn't mean we couldn't pounce if one of the guys got too drunk and passed out or mistreated the girl they were with.

I decided to just go with the flow that night and see what transpired. I made a conscious effort to curtail my drinking since I was driving and the road conditions were so treacherous. I won a few bucks at pool, had a slow dance with each of the Susies and a brief make-out session with Cathy Manning while her date went to the bathroom. Cathy was sort of an ex-girlfriend from Hathaway Brown that I'd dated off and on through my junior and senior years. She lived out in Pepper Pike and rode horses. I don't know if that made her hot, but that was the rumor. And she was hot, to a point. Hot enough for me to keep taking her out until I realized I was never going to get past that point. Our little five-minute tryst at the Coolidge party seemed like a goodbye and thanks for the memories.

When midnight hit, confetti was flying, the second keg was declared empty and everybody was kissing everybody. I kissed six or seven girls I had probably kissed sometime before in my high school career. Then they started with the slow classics: a Floyd Cramer instrumental, Ray Charles' *Georgia On My Mind*, Elvis's *Are You Lonesome Tonight*, The Drifters' *Save the Last Dance For Me*, and my favorite by The Platters, *Smoke Gets In Your Eyes*. Couples started pairing up, stags drifted together again and I could tell that the Coolidges were going to have this party wrapped up by 1:00 a.m. During *Unchained Melody* by The Righteous Brothers, Bob Lehmann (nickname: Bear), my other closest friend at US, came over to me.

"Lee, you gotta come help me with Dango."

"What's up?"

"He went kind of berserk at midnight. Couple of us had to hold him back from killing Muelenberg."

"He hit him?"

"No," Bob replied. "But it took Carlton and me both to hold him back. You know what an asshole Mule is, he was egging him on. Carleton wants Dango out of here."

"Where is he?"

"Out back. We got him into the garage."

We walked through the dancing couples to a small door leading to the four-car garage off the basement. This wasn't a house listed in Shaker Heights' most prestigious homes for nothing: the circular driveway curved in front of the home, and then there was a continuation off to the left that went down and around to the giant garage on the same level as the basement. Bob and I entered the garage and were hit with a blast of cold air. One of the carport doors had been opened. The garage was pitch-black. Outside all you could see was packed white snow on the driveway and the snow banks on either side where it had been cleared. Dango wasn't in the garage.

"Jesus," I said. "He's outside. Come on, let's get him."

"Lee," Bob said, grabbing my arm. "He took a swing at me. He's angry. He's drunk. I've got Janet inside. This needs to be you."

I knew he was right. There had been some other times when no one could talk to him but me.

"Okay, I got it," I said and headed for the lower driveway.

I walked out into the bitter cold and took a moment to let my eyes accustom to all the white. I didn't see him right away. I prayed he hadn't found his way up and around to the street, because if he wandered off the property in that condition and passed out, we'd never find him.

I heard what I thought at first was an animal cry or grunt. I turned and looked over to one of the eight-foot banks of cleared snow. In the bank was a dark indentation. I walked over. It was Dango, squatting in the bank like he had just been formed in a white plaster mold. It was the fetal position again, except not quite as tight as on the train, and not as peaceful. He was sobbing.

I walked over to him and put my hand on his shoulder. "Come on," I said. "It's time to go, the party's breaking up."

His bout of violence gone, he put his arm around my shoulder and leaned on me as we stumbled back to the garage.

"Why doesn't she love me, Lee?" he said, crying and whispering at the same time. "Why doesn't she love me?"

I had been the right one to go get him, because I was probably the only one that knew he wasn't talking about Muelenberg's date, Carol, or any other girl at the party. He was talking about his mother.

The train whistle brought me back from Cleveland. Our freight had sped up a bit since we were no longer climbing and I could tell we were passing through a sizable town. I guess the whistle was to inform anybody near the tracks at this hour that we weren't stopping. By standing on my tiptoes and pulling myself up, I could look over the edge of the car. I did that in time to see the Flagstaff station as we passed. Not a person was in sight.

The temperature had not dropped any further, my teeth were no longer chattering and I could feel my hands, so I headed over to the other corner by Dango, arranged my bags and quickly fell asleep.

I woke up because I was sweating. The sun was hitting the turbines, but I was still in the shaded corner. I looked over to Dango's corner, but he was gone. I slowly got up, stretched and heard him yell from the other end of the car.

"I'm down here."

I headed toward his voice into the sunlight and saw him zipping up his jeans. He'd just finished his morning piss in one of the far corners. He was back in his T-shirt.

"You're going to want to get those shirts off," he said.

"I figured that out the minute I woke up."

"We're back in the desert."

I took off my jacket and began unbuttoning the first of my shirts.

"How long to Albuquerque, do you think?"

"No idea," he answered. "But, I've been up about 10 minutes and we've been movin' along pretty good."

As far as Dango and I knew, Albuquerque was the only town in New Mexico. It certainly was the only town of any size on Route 66 in New Mexico. We assumed that the Santa Fe line followed Route 66. What we were soon to find out was that freight and passenger lines did not always coincide.

Once again, from what we could see over the high sides of the car, we were rolling through high desert Indian country. Not a town or home in sight, just the occasional pick-up truck bouncing down a dirt road, or a few rundown mobile homes with a car parked outside. The temperature climbed back up right along with the sun. At what we thought was about noon, we felt the freight begin to slow and we entered a sizable town

"Got to be Albuquerque," I said.

"Just in time. I'm starving and need something to drink," Dango replied.

"We'll eat something and get back on 66," I said. "Enough riding the rails."

Our train slowed some more and switched tracks, and suddenly we were surrounded by other freight cars. At a crawl now, we kept going for another five minutes, until we jerked to a stop. Looking over the side we couldn't see a station, just track after track of freight cars. We were in a big train yard, and from off in the distance, we could hear our engines disconnect. This was the end of the line for us, even if we'd wanted to stay on board.

I climbed out first and waited below as Dango passed out the bags. We started walking back toward the head of the train. We kept an eye out for the smelly occupants of the open boxcar, but they must have jumped out earlier because we never saw them again. As we trudged along with our luggage, we'd look left or right whenever there was a break in the cars to see if we could spot some kind of building or road. All we could see were more tracks, more freight cars. This was a huge train yard.

"Hey, I see some kind of opening up ahead," Dango shouted back.

Sure enough, we came to what looked like a small road through the yard that was kept clear of freight cars. To our left, up about five tracks, we spotted a couple of small wooden buildings next to an observation tower. We headed for them, thankful to have found any trace of civilization. To our amazement, one of the buildings had a small café. Too good to be true. We could get something to eat and drink, then get out of this maze back to 66.

We took our bags into the café with us. The signs I had painstakingly printed in Vegas were now in shreds. When we sat down at a table, I finished ripping them off. Two other tables in the restaurant were filled with men in jeans and baseball caps. Two other guys in the same uniform sat at the small counter. They were all eating, talking and laughing. They obviously all knew each other and worked for the railroad. When Dango and I entered, it quieted down as they watched us. Once again, we were completely out of place.

After we'd ordered a breakfast from the guy behind the counter, who was the cook, waiter and busboy rolled into one, I figured we'd better break the ice and get a little information.

"This is Albuquerque, right?" I asked the worker sitting nearest me at the table next to us.

That got a big laugh from all the other diners in the room.

"Nope. This is Belen," he answered.

Another guy, a little older, with a beard and dressed in jeans overalls, looking like the railroad worker stereotype, spoke next.

"You figuring to catch the Super Chief?" he said, gesturing to our bags.

That brought on another wave of laughter. I knew he was referencing the famous Santa Fe passenger train, and I also knew that they had us pegged for hopping the freight. Didn't stop Dango.

"No, we're hitchhiking. To Ohio. On Route 66."

That got a few more laughs, but also, I sensed a little respect.

"You're 25 or so miles south of Albuquerque and 66," one of the others offered.

At about that time, our food came and we stopped talking for about two minutes while we devoured it. The railroad men kept talking, looking over at us now and again and smiling. A couple of guys got up and left. With some energy restored, Dango and I began to discuss our dilemma. We were stuck in the middle of the largest train yard I'd ever seen. We'd have to find our way out, find the highway up to Albuquerque and hope there was enough traffic on it to get a lift. Here we were, the middle of day two out of Vegas, and it was looking like at least six days to get home. No way I could keep fooling my parents that we were on a Greyhound. I took out the map to find a route.

"You're looking for State 47," one of the guys at the table next to us said. "That'll take you right up to Albuquerque."

"Thanks," I said, and then turned back to the map.

As I was studying it, noticing how far we were from Cleveland and getting more and more disheartened, the café began to clear out. I guess their lunch break had finished. Only the bearded worker remained, nursing a cup of coffee and watching us.

"Ya know," he said. "It's almost two miles to 47 from here, that's assuming you can find your way out."

Dango and I nodded and looked at each other. What the hell was that supposed to be, helpful? Or was he just having more laughs at our expense? We must have appeared pretty pathetic, because he continued talking.

"The train on track 4's pulling out of here, headed east, in about 20 minutes. I'm sure there are a couple of empty cars."

With that, he got up and started to head out. Dango and I didn't waste a second. We jumped up, grabbed our bags and followed him.

Outside, I caught up to him first.

"Which one's track 4?"

"Count starts right here," he said, pointing to the track next to the buildings. "That's one, up that way's four."

"Thank you, sir," Dango said, as we headed in the direction he pointed.

"Watch out for the bull," he shouted after us.

"Bull?" Dango and I responded.

"Santa Fe Bull. Train cops."

Before Dango and I could ask him anything more, he disappeared into the yard. We had never heard of "train cops" and certainly hadn't seen any in our night-and-a-half-day of freight travel. If we'd given it any thought, we probably would have been a little worried about why they call them the "Santa Fe Bull," but we were too excited to be on our way again. Even if it was on another freight car.

We quickly reached track 4 and began searching for "our car." Didn't take long to find a fairly new looking B&O boxcar with an open door. It had a white notice posted on the outside, "Return for Service", with an east coast location for a Baltimore and Ohio yard. There was more handwriting under the "Return for Service" and since it was hard to make out, we didn't bother. Inside it was nice and clean, with absolutely nothing on its wood plank floor. Dango and I threw our bags in and hopped up to check it out. Perfect. We slid the door so it almost closed, leaving an opening of about a foot, so no one could see us. While Dango arranged our quarters, I slipped out to find something to wedge in the door opening. I don't know if it was a myth or not, but we'd heard stories of hoboes hopping freights, getting locked into boxcars and then their bodies being found six months later. That was not going to happen to these two smart, college-bound, Cleveland boys.

One track over, I found some broken-up wood pallets and was able to scrounge a three-foot length of two-by-four with a few small nails sticking out of it. I took it back to our boxcar and we hammered the nails into the wood flooring with our heels, leaving about four inches of the board peeking out of the door. Our safety secured, we sat back and waited for our next freight to pull out. After 20 minutes had passed, Dango and I began to worry that maybe we were on the wrong track, or that our friendly bearded guy in the overalls had set us up for another joke. Dango kept looking out the door to see if he could see some action up by the engine. Trouble was he couldn't see far enough to know where the engine was. After forty-five minutes, we were just about to pick up our bags when we heard the familiar sound of freight car couplings engaging coming towards us. Next thing we knew, we felt the jerk and we slowly started heading east. Dango and I sat down on the floor and smiled at each other.

"We could be all the way 'cross Texas tomorrow," Dango said confidently.

"Let's hope it's headed toward Oklahoma and not Arkansas," I replied, always trying to be the rational one.

"Lee, it's a B&O car, going back to some B&O yard. Why would it be headed south?"

"Hope you're right."

"Course I'm right. Relax."

So that's what I did. Truth was I was completely enjoying myself just like Dango. Not only had we hopped a freight in the middle of the Arizona desert, we'd hopped another in the middle of the biggest train yard I'd ever seen in New Mexico. With a little luck we could find ourselves hopping off tomorrow in St. Louis. No one, not one of our friends in Cleveland, had stories even close to this to tell.

It seemed to take forever getting out of the Belen train yard. The freight must have averaged between four and six mph as it switched tracks and crawled its way out. Compared to our open freight car, the ride in our spacious boxcar was almost luxurious. We had room to stretch out. We were warm and protected from the sun and wind. We could walk around when we felt like it, or stand by the partially open door and watch the scenery pass. It didn't bother us, at first, that the ride seemed a little bumpy.

Once we got out of town and the train began to pick up speed, the ride became worse. It was like driving over a rutted dirt road in a pick-up truck. It didn't bounce like our last ride in the Star Chief, just an irritating constant, bump, bump, bump. When the freight reached its cruising speed of about 45 mph the washboard ride didn't abate. After about 15 minutes, I turned to Dango.

"This must be a rough stretch of rail."

"Yeah, I was thinking the same thing. I thought all rails were smooth."

After another 20 minutes with no change, Dango asked the key question: "What did the notice say on the door of this car? Why's it being sent back for repairs?"

"I don't know." I said. "There was some handwritten stuff under

'Return for Service' and I didn't read it."

"I'm gonna go read it." Dango said.

"It's on the outside of the door."

"I know. Help me."

We opened the sliding door so Dango could just get through. There was a very slight lip on the outside edge of the door, where his PF Flyers could get a little purchase. Grabbing hold of the outside door handle with his left hand, leaving his left foot on the boxcar floor and putting his right foot as far out on the lip as he could, he was able to stretch his right arm toward the notice.

"Can you read it?" I shouted, holding on to his left wrist with both hands.

"No," he shouted back. "But I got an idea. When I yell 'Now,' pull me back in."

With that, I felt him stretch a little further then I heard paper ripping and then "Now!"

He came around the edge of the door, his right arm and leg floating in space outside the car for a second, before he fell on top of me to the floor. He held most of the notice in his right hand. It had ripped right through the center of "Return for Service," but had the handwriting and a date. There were only three handwritten words, they were kind of hard to make out, but once we did, it might have been expected: "Suspension Shot – Replace." Dango and I read it, looked at each other, bumping along on the floor of that boxcar and started to laugh. God had found a most appropriate way to punish us for running away from responsibility and deserting our faithful Pontiac.

"I didn't know railroad cars had suspension. Did you?" I asked.

"I do ... do ... do ... no ... no ... now," he answered.

We laughed again, but that was the last time as we settled into our train ride through New Mexico and purgatory. There was no finding comfort. You could only sit for short periods. We would take turns standing by the door, looking out and watching the empty

New Mexico landscape pass. We couldn't appreciate the beauty of the wild country, because it only seemed to reinforce the growing realization on our part that we had miles to go before we could get off this thing. As dusk came, there was still no civilization in sight.

"Can't you get kidney damage from constant shaking?" Dango asked.

"I think we're young enough, so we're okay. Train's gotta stop someplace."

"Are you sure?"

Night came. We'd look out the door and not see a light. It took hours for minutes to pass. I had a watch that I'd forgotten to wind and we'd probably crossed another time zone, so we had no idea how late or early it was when we finally felt the train begin to slow. We were entering a town of some size.

"Do you think it's Amarillo?" Dango asked.

"I don't care what it is," I answered. "We're getting off."

The second the train stopped, we jumped off, bags in hand. It was another freight yard. A few lights high up on poles cast an eerie, dim light overall and created dark shadows from the parked railroad cars. If we hadn't been traveling for god-knows-how many hours, I would have sworn we were still in Belen. We started walking to find a way out, the romance of "riding the rails" left far behind us somewhere in the Arizona desert.

Through breaks in the freight cars, we could make out lights of what seemed like buildings off to our right; we headed that way, climbing up and over couplings if we had to, to get across the tracks. At last we reached the end of the tracks and a 50-yard stretch of gravel-covered ground was all that lay between us and a chain-link fence. There was an open gate in the fence leading to buildings, a dark road and parked cars. I didn't realize how much I missed automobiles and roads until that second. As tired and "shaken" as we were, we picked up our pace.

"Halt!"

A bright beam of light hit us and the big voice sounded again.

"Stop right there!"

Dango and I immediately did as we were told. We set our bags down. I thought for a second about putting my hands up, but instead, just turned to look at what was coming.

In the dim light and when the beam of the large flashlight was not directly in my eyes, I could make out two men coming toward us. The one who seemed to be in charge was holding the flashlight and wore some kind of khaki uniform with a wide-brimmed, highway patrol hat. The other man was smaller and held tightly to the leash of large, vicious-looking Rottweiler. I knew immediately that we were looking at a Santa Fe Bull. I also knew immediately, how they got the name "Bull."

The guy in the uniform was the stereotype of the stereotypical Southern sheriff. He was 5'10 inches tall and built like a fireplug. I never saw under the hat, but you just knew he had a crew cut or shaved his head. He was a dead-ringer for Sheriff Bull Conner of Birmingham, Alabama, who would become infamous during the civil rights marches in 1963. He looked just like Rod Steiger in the Oscar winning movie, *In the Heat of the Night*. He was built like a bull, acted like a bull and, if bulls could talk, talked like a bull.

"What are you doing here?" he shouted in our faces.

I was scared to silence. All I could do was stare at the badge on his khaki shirt – "Santa Fe RR Police."

Somehow Dango responded, "Looking for a place to stay, sir."

"What?" he barked. "You're trespassing on private property. This is a Santa Fe Railroad yard. How'd you get here?"

"I don't know, sir," Dango went on, winging it. "We've been hitchhiking and were asleep and this fellow just dropped us off."

God, you had to admire Dango for that. What fast thinking under duress. Don't admit to having been on a train, let them prove it.

"He's right, sir," I said, picking up the ball. "We're hitching all the way to Ohio. This is Amarillo, isn't it?"

The guy holding tight to the dog laughed. The "bull" gave him a look that could kill and then turned his disgust back to us.

"You are two of the dumbest deadbeats, I've ever seen. You just got off that freight that just pulled in, didn't you?"

"No sir," we both said at the same time.

"We're looking for a place to stay," Dango continued, gesturing to our bags.

"How old are you?"

"Eighteen, sir."

"Get the fuck out of here now," he growled. "Before I let this dog eat you."

"Yes sir," we said, picking up our bags as fast as we could and heading toward the opening in the fence.

"And," he shouted after us. "Welcome to Clovis, New Mexico, you dumb shits."

We could hear them behind us cracking themselves up. We didn't turn around to look.

CHAPTER 5

Clovis to Amarillo

After we left the train yard, we kept moving as fast as we could with our bags. I just knew the Santa Fe Bull would let the Rottweiler loose for fun. When we cleared the first block, we turned a corner and hit the main "downtown" section of Clovis. It was just one short street of shops, restaurants and businesses. Not a soul was in sight at whatever hour we'd arrived. Other than two or three low-wattage streetlights, the only other light was a neon "Hotel" sign above the door of the largest building on the block. From a horror movie scene in Seligman to a '40s grade B gangster movie scene in Clovis, our evening stops on this cross-country adventure had lots of room for improvement. Dango and I were so tired and scared from our train ride and brush with the law, we didn't notice or care what the place looked like. We entered the hotel and paid an unusually thin night clerk at the desk $14 plus tax for a fourth floor room. We took the rickety elevator up, threw our bags on the floor, relieved ourselves in a toilet for a change, stripped down to our shorts and collapsed into our beds. Before I fell asleep, I glanced at the cheap clock on the nightstand – it was only 11:30 p.m.

I woke up to a rooster crowing and Dango snoring. It was still dark. For a good minute I didn't know where I was. Then it came back to me, a dingy room on the fourth floor of a hotel in Clovis, New Mexico. That meant I still didn't know where I was. I had never heard of Clovis and I had not looked at my map after we escaped the train yard last night.

I got up quietly, removed the map from my bag and went over to the small cheap wooden desk on the wall across from the beds. There was no TV in the room. I turned on the desk lamp and spread out the map. In eight hours of freight travel, which seemed more like 20 hours, we had only managed to cover about 250 miles. I didn't bother to calculate the train speed, but Dango and I had been way high thinking it was 45 mph. Although Clovis was right on the Texas border, we hadn't even left New Mexico or broken into another time zone. We had also drifted southeast while Route 66 had headed a little northwest. We were about 50 miles directly south of the renowned east-west highway. The only good news – there was a direct route leading up to Amarillo, which was only 150 miles away: Route 60.

Early morning gray light was now coming in the window. I turned to wake Dango so we could get an early start and to give him the disappointing news about our location. The snoring had stopped; he had kicked off most of his covers and was lying on his back with a big grin on his face. It dawned on me that Dango was, at that moment, happy wherever he was. I was the one always checking the map to see how far we'd gotten or where we were. Dango never even looked at the map. He didn't care where we were. He was out of his house and on the road; that was good enough for him.

It also occurred to me that not only had Dango not looked at the map since we left Sequoia, but he had not talked to his parents either. At least I didn't think he had. Teenagers are so into themselves that they can be oblivious to the dynamics of relationships within their own family. When it comes to having any insight into what goes on in other families – not a clue.

I knew one thing – Dango didn't get along with his mother. I figured that out when we first became friends in junior high school. Whenever we'd go over to his place, and she was home, she'd always be ragging on him for something or another. Then there was the time in our sophomore year at US when I spent two weeks at Dango's house while my parents went to Europe.

Dango's room was in the attic while his mom, dad, older sister and younger brother had rooms on the second floor of the Delaware house. His whole family was terrific with me, including his mom, Elaine. The rest of them seemed to get along fine with Dango, too. But between Dango and Elaine you could always feel the tension and it never took much for it to break into the open. To Dango's friends she was known as the mother with the "Two Ts", a temper and a tongue.

Twice during my stay in 1959, we had run-ins with his mother that left me very uncomfortable. Both were when we returned from US late in the afternoon. Each time, Elaine went off on him the moment we entered the house, so I had no chance to escape the tirade and had to stand silently next to my taller friend. I don't remember why she was so upset; a bad grade he got, something she heard he had done at school, or something he hadn't done at home. Whatever it was, she'd use that rapier-like tongue to chop Dango up in front of me. He would take it all, just looking at her without saying a word. At the end of each one of these outbursts, she looked over at me and then back to him and say something like, "Why don't you be more like Lee?" or, "Lee wouldn't do that. Would you?" I cringed and said something in Dango's defense, but that was the end of it and we were dismissed. Later, up in his room, Dango would say it didn't bother him, that he'd stopped listening. He never said to me, "She doesn't mean it."

It was crazy to think that anyone would want Dango to be more like me. Looking at him now, sound asleep in this dingy hotel room, I realized that I wished I was more like him. Why did I have to be the worrier? Why couldn't I attack every new day with Dango's confidence? Who was the leader on this expedition? It certainly wasn't me.

Maybe almost getting kicked out of US my last semester had made me more cautious? Maybe having older parents made a difference? Dango's parents were young. My dad was 61 in '61, my mom 56. Dango's parents were struggling to get ahead, mine were already there. Dango had an angry mom, I had a type-A dad – which in my mind meant he was always ready to blow his stack. Any way you looked at it, we were both 18 years old and the less interaction we had with our parents the better. As far as we were concerned, neither set of parents knew a thing about what we were going through.

Yet, the incident at US the last semester of my senior year did give me a whole new outlook on my dad. And maybe gave me a reason to pause before I just jumped in and did something crazy that looked like a good idea at the time. For once, Dango wasn't involved.

Bob Lehmann and I wrote the social column for the University School newspaper and had a lot of fun doing it. In fact, we had more fun doing it than we should have, because we had created a way to sneak secret messages to the troops right under the nose of the faculty adviser. We'd write short little poems describing various events that happened during the school year and use the first letter of each line to pass on other important information. Earlier in the year, our acrostics had exhorted the faithful to "DRINK BUD" or "BREW IT UP." For the last edition of the spring semester, reporting on the antics of the New Year festivities during and after Coolidge's party, we decided to go all-out for our fans and wrote the following:

> *Four o'clock called*
> *Upon us at Dave's*
> *Could anyone there*
> *Keep back his wild raves?*

Your evening had been good:
Odds favored a good time.
Upon this last thought,
All wish to close this here rhyme.

Lest no one remain for the next column, however.
Let us now take leave of our brave, bold endeavor.

"Stupid endeavor" would have been more like it. I remember going to the University School basketball game the Friday evening the paper came out and seeing the kids passing copies through the stands, pointing to the column and laughing. No way someone in the faculty wasn't going to find out about our semester-ending blessing. Turned out to be worse than a faculty member; some lower-class man showed it to his Cleveland society grandmother and the US headmaster had a full-blown scandal brewing by the weekend. Lehmann and I were called into the headmaster's office on Monday and suspended while proper punishment was being deliberated. Expulsion was expected for such an offense.

Now, besides being poets and "rebels without a cause," Lehmann and I had a couple of points in our favor. We were both elected senior members of the student council, got good grades and had applied to prestigious colleges. Lehmann was undoubtedly the smartest student in all of University School: perfect scores on his SATs and National Merit Scholarship tests, all A's throughout high school and penciled in to go to Harvard. Since he never studied very hard, the term "genius" was thrown around when other classmates talked about him. I was planning on going to Princeton. I was definitely only borderline Princeton material, but, once again, I had pull. The Princeton representative for the Cleveland area worked directly under my dad at the large engineering firm downtown where my dad was on the board of directors.

In the week when our futures were being discussed, Lehmann and I were left out of the proceedings. It was in the hands of the headmaster, faculty members, US alumni and our parents. The ruling on Lehmann came down first: he was expelled and would have to spend his final semester of high school in public school in Pepper Pike. Interesting to note here, academic prowess obviously played no part in the decision. Lehmann's parents were relatively new German immigrants and had no social standing whatsoever in Cleveland Heights/Shaker Heights society. He never did get into Harvard.

My father handled the negotiations for our family. My mother, whom I had been closest to throughout my school years, could do little more than cry. She saw my future in ruins. The evening of the final decision my parents took me up to University School, and while they were in the headmaster's office, I was left alone in the large study hall. All the lights were on, which I remember thinking was overkill for a solitary student sitting in the middle of 100 or so desks. Outside it was black and white – nighttime with fresh snow covering the trees, roadways and athletic fields. I had no one to talk to, no book, not even a pad of paper to doodle on. It was like that moment of realization when I drove off the road on the way up to Sequoia that I had really screwed up, except this seemed to last for hours.

When my father came to get me after what I believe now was only about 20 minutes, he walked over to where I was sitting. I looked up at him to try and read his face. He was dressed in his best business suit, having come straight from work to pick us up and attend the meeting. He still wore his fedora, even inside.

"They're going to let you stay and finish," he said. "But, they're going to take their pound of flesh."

I stood up. He put his two hands on my shoulder and looked me in the eyes.

"You're on probation. You come to school, attend classes and come home immediately after. You're stripped of being a class officer, yearbook editor and newspaper associate editor. No extra-curricular stuff. You'll have a black mark on your transcript. Forget Princeton."

I took a deep breath and thought for a second about crying. Then he hugged me to him in one arm and spoke softly close to my face.

"And let me tell you something else: These are the biggest bunch of fucking hypocrites I've ever seen in my life. In a few years, it'll mean exactly what it is – nothing."

After that, I did cry. I cried not because of what had been done to me, but because I discovered I had a father who loved me no matter what I did. Funny, at eighteen, to come to that realization.

Funny, to sit in a depressing hotel room in Clovis, New Mexico, looking at my sleeping best friend and begin to comprehend that he did not have the same certainty with his parents. I decided to let him sleep a little longer, so I got up from the desk, went into the very small bathroom and took a long shower.

When we finally exited the hotel the sun was up and it was 7:15 a.m. The downtown of Clovis in the morning didn't have much more color than it did at night. Instead of gray, it was sort of overall beige. We crossed the street to a small café/coffee shop to get some breakfast. Once again, two teenage boys carrying suitcases were as out of place as whites at Gleason's Musical Bar. Locals who looked to be mostly farmers or ranchers all watched us as we came in and walked over to a small booth. A heavy-set waitress in her 40s, wearing no make-up but a smile, brought us some plastic-covered single-page menus.

"Where you boys headed?" she asked as she set the menus on the table.

"Cleveland, Ohio," I said.

"We're hitchhiking," Dango added.

"No way," she exclaimed. "How in the hell did you all end up in Clovis?"

"We hopped a freight in Arizona," Dango continued. "And this is where it dropped us off."

I probably would not have gone into all that detail, but Dango's openness made the whole restaurant want to hear the story. When we told about the Clovis train yard and the Santa Fe Bull, everybody seemed to get a good laugh out of it.

"Yep, that sounds like Jerry Carter," an older guy at the counter offered. "Was he wearing his gun?"

I looked at Dango. "Boy, I didn't see one, just that big flashlight."

"Well, you're lucky," he went on. "He's got a big old Colt 45 he wears sometimes. Scares the hell out of the bums with it."

"We were scared enough with the dog," Dango said.

"Oh that's just Buster," the waitress said. "Looks like a killer, but he's a pussycat."

The open forum continued all during our breakfast of corned beef hash and eggs. Everyone in the café joined in with advice and stories. Jerry Carter, apparently, was not high on anyone's list of favorite people.

Judy, the waitress, found me some big brown wrapping paper, a large black magic marker and some adhesive tape, so I was able to re-create our "Students" and "Ohio" signs. Ken, the older guy at the counter, insisted on buying us breakfast (less than four bucks total) and driving us out to Route 60, a few miles out of town to the east. While in his pick-up on the short drive, it occurred to me that having two crazy teenagers from Cleveland pass through their town might have been worthy of a couple of days news in Clovis. Good for a chuckle at the café, or bar, or around the dinner table for a week or two.

Setting up our bags at the intersection of the road from Clovis and 60, after Ken had dropped us off, I could understand why our appearance might cause some excitement. There was nothing to see for miles except a very straight two-lane highway headed northeast, a line of phone poles alongside it and flat, flat land as far as the eye could see. It reminded me of the intersection where Cary

Grant almost got killed by the crop duster in Hitchcock's *North by Northwest*, except there were no crops. Didn't seem to be many cars either.

A couple of semis passed carrying cattle, an oil tanker barreled by, and then an old pick-up with Mexican laborers in the back. Dango and I began to worry that maybe no cars ever traveled this road. But only 10 minutes had passed in what would turn out to be the biggest mileage day of our trip. Our good luck began with the first car that we saw on 60 – a blue and white '57 Chevy Bel Air convertible.

It approached from the Clovis road and, as soon as the driver saw us, began to slow. It pulled to the shoulder of 60 a few feet past us, stopped and a young guy in khaki slacks and button-down shirt got out. "Come on," he said, "I'm going to Amarillo."

First car – 150 miles. He opened the trunk, we put our bags in and then we took our seats. Dango in back, me shotgun. If you're any kind of American car buff, you know what a collector's treasure a '57 Chevy Bel Air in good shape is now. In 1961, to teens and young men, it already had the beginning of that mystique. Only the coolest guys drove '57 Bel Airs. Even if they weren't cool, you gave them credit for being cool if they had a '57 Bel Air. The guy driving this one matched up to the car. He had short-cropped blonde hair, good physique and looked to be in his twenties. On a hanger over the driver's side back window was a blue Air Force uniform. I couldn't make out the rank.

"You're in the Air Force?" I asked.

"Yeah, stationed at Cannon, big base just south of Clovis."

"Now I know why Clovis exists," Dango said from the back.

Our driver laughed. "Spent some time in Clovis, have you?"

"A little," I said.

"Well, Cannon's not Clovis's only claim to fame."

"There's something else?" Dango asked.

"Big railroad town and Buddy Holly."

"Buddy Holly?"

"Yup. Buddy Holly's hometown."

"Now we know why he left," Dango said.

We drove in silence. I looked out over the hood to where the two little finned rocket points shot forward. I knew they were matched in back by the two straight-line tail fins that cut back into the body. In the model years after the '57, tail fins and hood paraphernalia would go crazy on all cars. The '57 Bel Air was the master of perfect understatement. After about five minutes, our driver broke the silence.

"Hey, my name is Steve, by the way. What are your names?"

"I'm Lee," I answered. "That's Bob, or Dango."

"Dango? What the hell's Dango?"

"His nickname."

With that, we got into how Dango got his name, Cleveland and Shaker Heights, Ohio and Steve's growing up in Amarillo. He made sure to join the Air Force, because he really wanted out of Amarillo. He asked where we were going to college and what we wanted to do afterwards. Neither Dango nor I could give him much of an answer. We hadn't given much thought to anything past our last summer in Cleveland.

The miles wore on. The monotony of the road without curves and the barren landscape on either side of it got to me, so I asked Steve a question that had been on my mind since I'd seen his uniform.

"So, are you a pilot?"

"Yeah," he said. "As a matter of fact, I am."

"How long have you been in the Air Force?"

"I started my freshman year at Texas, Air Force ROTC."

"You started flying then?"

"Oh, hell no. Did a little private flying to get the basics. But I got my real flight training at Lackland in San Antonio after I graduated."

"You fly jets?" I asked.

I don't know what I was thinking. All I knew about jets was some movie I'd seen in the fifties called *The Bridges at Toko-Ri*, where William Holden had flown Sabre jets in the Korean War.

"Yep, but not fighters. Mainly big transports like the C-130. I ship out to Korea next month," Steve said.

"I thought Korea was over," said Dango.

"Since '56," he replied. "But it's just an armistice. We still have planes up everyday waiting for it to get hot again. And we'll be transporting supplies to other areas in Southeast Asia."

"Southeast Asia?" I asked, not having any idea what he was talking about. There was nothing in the news around that time that had anything to do with Southeast Asia. From what little I read or heard on TV, most international stuff that summer had to do with Castro and Cuba, Khrushchev and the USSR. Kennedy was getting beat up his first year in office.

"Yeah, we have some small contingents of Green Berets in Laos and Vietnam," Steve said. "Those seem to be a couple of hot spots."

"What are Green Berets?" Dango asked from the backseat, before I could ask it myself.

"Special highly trained army forces," Steve replied. "Kinda like commandos, I guess."

"So, what is it going to be - another war or something?" Dango said.

"Oh, I don't think so," he replied. "Only 400 of these guys went into Vietnam earlier this year to help train the South Vietnamese army."

"It's a North/South thing again?" I asked. "Like Korea?"

He started to chuckle. "Don't ask me, guys. I'm just going to be taking 'em supplies. I just do what I'm ordered."

That was the end of that conversation. He didn't seem to want to talk any more about it and it didn't seem like anything important to Dango and me. I took a look around. Nothing had changed. The road still hadn't turned and only a few cars had passed us heading the opposite direction.

Two things on the drive broke the monotony of the flat terrain – occasional herds of cattle and a small forest of oil wells every 20 or 30 miles. Steve explained that Amarillo was basically a cattle town, with oil being its secondary reason for existence. Of course, it was also the only town in Texas of any size on Route 66. Even knowing that didn't prepare you for how much 66 seemed to dominate all the activity in Amarillo.

We entered the outskirts on Route 60. On either side of us was block after block of one-story ranch-style homes. We were struck by the lack of trees and how flat everything was. The homes disappeared once we turned on to 66. You would have sworn you were back in Vegas by the array of large, gaudy, blinking signs on either side of the road. Except there were no casinos. The signs all had western themes – cowboys tipping their 12-gallon hats, Indian Chiefs in full headdress, galloping horses, teepees and masked bandits. As far as I could tell, they only seemed to be advertising four businesses – motels, gas stations, "authentic" western gear and steak houses. I never saw so many steak houses on one stretch of road in my life. I guess by the time people heading west on Route 66 hit Amarillo after hundreds of miles of seeing nothing but flatland, cattle and oil wells, they had to have a steak.

"I'll drop you guys on the east end of town," Steve said. "Then head back to my parent's place."

"Thanks for everything," I said, then turned to wake Dango, who had dozed off in back the last few miles before Amarillo.

Steve pulled off on the shoulder just past the last gas station on the eastbound side. You could see a small radio station with a giant radio tower next to it about 220 yards or so ahead then just 66 heading straight to its vanishing point over more flat prairie.

After Steve opened the trunk so we could reclaim our bags, the three of us shook hands.

"Thanks for the lift," I said. "And good luck overseas."

"Hey, good luck to you guys," he said. "Lotta road left 'til Cleveland."

With that he waved, got back in the Bel Air, looked both ways on 66 and then crossed the yellow line and started back into Amarillo. I remember watching as the Bel Air disappeared into the confusion of cars, big semis and busy road signs, and being envious of Steve's sense of purpose. He certainly knew what direction he was headed. I turned back to Dango, who had already set up the bags to be easily read by traffic leaving town. He was now standing gazing at the distant radio tower.

"You know," he said. "We haven't had a beer since we left Las Vegas."

I knew immediately what had made him miss our daily beer.

"We don't have time for a climb," I said jokingly.

"I know," he replied. "Just with all this flat land, we could probably see all the way to Oklahoma."

"You're up," I said, as I sat down on a small patch of grass off the shoulder.

Dango broke his gaze from the tower, stuck out his thumb and began the first round of hitchhiking. He stood tall, shoulders back with a smile on his face, trying to look every bit the clean cut, friendly and harmless student our sign promised. If drivers only knew his penchant for finding new and more dangerous places to drink beer - places like the top of radio towers - they'd never stop.

So much of our high school weekend time in Cleveland, if truth be known, was spent driving around trying to figure out what to do. Only occasionally did we have dates, or parties to go to, or a game to attend. Most evenings we were just looking for some place to hang out, drink some beers and talk. Trouble was, since we were underage, we could only do that at someone's house if the parents weren't home. Parking out by the Chagrin River was fine in the afternoon, but after dark you might drive off the bank and end up in the river. Dango and his other best buddy, Big John AuWerter, came up with the radio tower concept one summer evening before our senior year. All you needed was an old newspaper bag.

Just about every male teenager in the Heights had delivered newspapers during junior high school. Riding your bike and flipping papers into the doorways of the giant homes was the perfect way for 10- to 14-year-olds to earn a little money. I had delivered the afternoon paper in my Cleveland Heights neighborhood for two years and even though I only had about 36 homes over six blocks, I had to cover three square miles of area. This all connects to climbing radio towers and drinking beers because of the bags we used to carry the papers. Large canvas shoulder bags with a flap stenciled with the name of whichever Cleveland daily you delivered: the morning "Plain Dealer," or the afternoon "Press" or "News."

The bags, it turned out, were perfect for carrying a six-pack of beer, on ice, while you climbed the "tiny" ladder on the side of the tower up to the "tiny" platform just under the final beacon. How and why John and Dango ever came up with this beer drinking post I can only surmise: No one would ever think to look for underage teenagers drinking at the top of a radio tower. It was against the law and definitely had an element of danger attached to it. And once you were there at the top, you could look out at the whole world. The same sort of reasoning went into Dango and my choosing Moro Rock for our afternoon beers at Sequoia.

I joined Dango and John one summer evening. I think other friends joined them at other times, but it really was a drinking spot best suited for two. Only two could squeeze into the small platform at the top. The third party had to hang on to the ladder with one arm while enjoying his brew with his free hand – a little spooky when you were almost 600 feet above Cleveland. I did it once, and then figured I'd search for my kicks a little closer to the ground.

Dango and John found about four different radio towers in various suburbs around Cleveland where they could indulge their favorite pastime and satisfy their urge for danger. On their twelfth tower-climbing escapade, they decided to do it on a snowy winter weekend. Winter climbing had only one advantage – they didn't have to buy ice. They packed beer and snow in their newspaper shoulder bags and climbed the icy ladder in heavy winter jackets, gloves and boots. The particular tower they chose that night overlooked an intersection on Ohio Route 17 in the Cleveland suburb of Brook Park, about five miles east of the airport, south of downtown.

When Dango related the tale of this winter adventure to me the next week at school, he explained that the cold weather forced them to do new things once they reached the top. If you just sat and talked and enjoyed the view, like in the summertime, you'd freeze. So to keep active and somewhat warm, they decided to throw snowballs at the cars passing far below on Route 17.

It was not only fun, Dango related, but required great skill because they had to calculate how long the snowball took to hit the road from the top of the tower, and match it to the length of time it took for cars to leave the intersection light and reach that point in the road where the snowballs landed. Advanced artillery training 101. It took them 10 snowballs until they hit their first car. John and Dango toasted their bullseye with another cold beer.

The third car they hit was a cop car. Dango said it must have hit like a rock, because those cops were so mad, they spent 10 minutes searching the sides of the road for who threw it. When they found John's parents' station wagon parked by the side of Route 17 and saw the foot tracks in the snow leading to the radio tower, John and Dango knew they were dead. The police used the searchlight on their car to pan up the tower and illuminate the two teenagers with no place to hide. They used their bullhorn to issue orders.

"You up there, come down now! Slowly, so we can see you."

Dango always said he thought the "so we can see you" was a little overly dramatic.

"There was no way to come down where they couldn't see us," he said.

He also let me know he and John had left all the beer cans, empty and full, up at the top. No matter what other laws we broke, we University School boys weren't going to get caught for underage drinking.

"Stop right there – at the bottom of the tower."

That was the last order from the bullhorn, as the two Cleveland policemen walked over through the snow to cuff John and Dango. Dango said he thought it was all over, that he and John were sure to spend the night in jail. After that, they would spend the rest of their senior year in public school.

The cops brought them over to the squad car parked next to the station wagon. They got the boys' names, ages and home addresses. Then the senior officer went over to the police car and called it in. The other younger officer pointed out to Dango and John the six prominent "Private Property," "No Trespassing" and "Danger" signs they had managed to ignore. Dango said he made it sound like prison for sure. After taking quite a while calling in the violation, the senior officer came over and conferred with his partner. Then he walked over to where John and Dango stood, their hands cuffed behind their backs.

"Turn around!" he shouted.

John and Dango did as they were told. The officer took his key and un-cuffed them.

"Turn around and listen."

John and Dango again did as they were told - and I know all this because Dango gave it to me word for word.

"I'm not taking you in," the cop said, spitting the words through his teeth. "I'm not taking you in because you're two boys from the Heights, and if I booked you, it'd be all over the papers and then we'd have kids from all over Cleveland climbing these damn things. But if you ever get caught on another tower, even close to one, we got your name downtown and it's straight to jail. Now get out of here. Go back to the Heights and stay there."

Dango and John never did do it again. Neither did anyone else for that matter. The novelty was gone. But there was something to it, especially for Dango. Some reason why we felt we had to break the boredom of the early '60s by drinking beer and taking chances.

"Your turn," said Dango, kicking me in the leg while I sat on my little grass patch by the side of Route 66.

"Do a few more."

"One more," he said, as he turned and held out his thumb for a single Cadillac coming out of Amarillo.

"Cadillacs never stop," I said.

Just as I said it, the big car pulled off on the shoulder right in front of us and stopped. It was a brand new white Cadillac Eldorado with a man and a woman inside; Texas plates and longhorns on the grille.

CHAPTER 6

Amarillo to Tulsa

The couple opened both front doors of the Eldorado and exited at the same time. For a second, they stood by their respective doors. Dango and I stood by our bags and we just looked at each other. Dango and I didn't move, because we were stunned. Facing us was one of the fanciest cars on the road and one of the oddest couples I had ever seen. The man stood about 5'9", in black cowboy boots, jeans and a Western shirt with sleeves rolled up. He was stocky, muscular, had short-cropped black hair and a big smile. The woman wore flats, tight white jeans, a loose sequined sweater, and looked to be about six feet tall. Her hair was fairly long and definitely bleached blonde. Her face showed many miles but even the loose sweater couldn't hide that she was packing some Blaze Starr hardware. I figured them to be in their late forties.

The man broke the awkward silence.

"How you boys doing?" he said, as he left his door and came toward us with his right hand extended. "I'm Ron Shanks and this is Joanna."

"Hi, I'm Lee," I said, shaking his hand and then gesturing to Dango. "This is Bob."

"We're heading on up to Tulsa today," Ron said. "Want to come along?"

"Sure do," I replied. "Don't we, Bob?"

I elbowed Dango to get his attention and break his fixation on Joanna's sweater.

"That'd be great," Dango said, snapping out of it. "Should I put our bags in the trunk?"

"Absolutely," Ron replied. "C'mon."

He headed toward the back of the Eldorado, keys in hand and Dango followed, somehow carrying all four bags and looking like a young Samson. Joanna's eyes followed him.

Since I was standing there with nothing to do, I turned to her and said, "Hi." She looked at me with a little smile and said "Hi" in return. Except, I swear, her 'Hi' took about 10 seconds to get out and seemed to carry with it all kinds of other messages.

"Listen," Ron said as he and Dango returned to the front of the car from stowing the bags. "You guys drive, right? You have licenses?"

"Yes, Sir," I answered.

"Good, 'cause I've been driving all day and if we're gonna reach Tulsa, I'll need to take a break."

"Well, I drove a '56 Pontiac," I said. "Almost the same size as this thing. So, I'll be glad to give it a shot."

"Great," Ron replied. "Why don't you get in front with me? Bob, you ride in back with Joanna and we'll get this show on the road."

So that's exactly what we did and that's exactly what it was, all 350 miles to Tulsa – a "show."

There are some people in life that the first time you meet them, they let you know their whole life story. These people don't live in Shaker or Cleveland Heights, Ohio. So Ron Shanks was the first one I'd ever met. From the moment he started driving the first leg from Amarillo to Oklahoma City, the conversation never stopped. And Ron did most of the talking.

I don't remember exactly how the conversation started but it probably had something to do with the Eldorado. The Cadillac was filled with all kinds of goodies that no car I saw in the '60s ever had. First off, in back, they had rigged up some kind of small TV with antenna. The only small TVs they had in those days were black-and-whites with rabbit-ear antenna that you might see on a kitchen counter. Somehow Ron had rigged one off of a DC converter that would play in the car. Ron said he did it so Joanna would not have to miss *This Is Your Life* when they were on the road, which as we would learn, was quite often. I had been forced to watch *This Is Your Life* with my grandmother in Cleveland and, along with *Queen for a Day*, it was one of the shows that teenagers would avoid at all costs and for which the word "Schmaltz" was invented.

Underneath the dash was a built-in 45 record player. The spindle hung upside down, so that the arm with needle actually played the record upside down. It was all suspended with springs somehow, so that as you rolled along on the road it would play without skipping. We played a few records. Joanna had all of Elvis's 45s, and it worked pretty well especially with the smooth ride of the Eldorado on the stretch of 66 from Amarillo to the Oklahoma line. It was far from perfect, however, and a bump would cause the needle to skip. The TV couldn't pick up any stations in the sparsely populated area between Amarillo and Oklahoma City, either.

These were just expensive toys in an expensive car, and that's probably what prompted Dango's direct open question, "So, Ron, how did you make all your money?"

"Wildcatting," he answered. "Made my first million wildcatting, then lost it, then made it back. Lost it again then met Joanna and got smart."

"You just stopped drinking," Joanna piped in from the back seat.

"That's part of it," Ron said. "Stopped gambling, too. See, Joanna's my bookkeeper. She showed me wildcatting's a form of gambling. So, once I hit my last well, I sold and got out of it."

"How'd you get into wildcatting in the first place?" I asked.

"Met a good ol' boy in Leavenworth who was a wildcatter. He showed me the ropes when I got out."

"Leavenworth?" Dango and I said.

"Why were you in Leavenworth?" I asked.

"Oh, it happened way back when I was just 19 in Tennessee. I shot a guy."

"You killed him?"

"Yup. He cheated me and my mom outta some money, so I went to get it back. My dad was dead. We were dirt poor. The bastard laughed at me, so I shot him. Not sure I meant to kill him, but I did. The jury ended up convicting me for 2nd degree murder. Almost got manslaughter. They knew he was a bastard. Anyway, off to Leavenworth, got out in eight years with good behavior."

While he was talking, I looked back at Dango, he looked at me, our eyes widened; we were not sure if we should have taken this ride or not. Riding in a car with someone who had shot someone dead and had spent time in one of the most notorious maximum-security prisons in the country was even further from the Cleveland/Shaker Heights experience than hopping a freight train. The more Ron talked, however, the more comfortable we became. Everything he said to us was in the same matter-of-fact, no bullshit, perfectly normal tone of voice. He never raised his voice or got angry. In fact, most of the time it was with a smile. He loved telling his story to complete strangers.

Joanna would pipe in occasionally from the backseat to embellish something or gently tease him, but the conversation was all Ron's.

It was shortly after we started off that I noticed the tattoos on Ron's hands. Beneath the knuckle on each finger, on each hand, one letter was tattooed. On the right hand the letters were L-O-V-E, on the left hand, H-A-T-E. He told me those were the first tattoos he'd gotten in Leavenworth. Joanna told us he had more all over his body. Her favorites were the HOT and COLD, one above each nipple. You couldn't say that Ron didn't have a sense of humor.

"So, you started wildcatting right after you got out of Leavenworth," I started the conversation up again, wanting to steer it away from prison.

"My good friend that had gotten out earlier worked for a wildcatter all over Texas and Oklahoma. I worked with him, and after a couple of years, we put together a small stake and went out on our own."

"It's awful tough, though," he went on. "Most all the promising land has already been leased by the big oil companies. You end up searching in areas that they've overlooked or given up on. We made one strike, sold it to Texaco and kept a royalty. They pumped it out in two years."

"But you made a fortune when you sold it, didn't you?" Dango asked.

"Hey, did real well," Ron replied. "But half went to Johnny, my buddy. He'd had enough and went down to Galveston and got married. So I went back to doing it on my own with a small crew."

"That's Ron," Joanna said. "Never give up. Stubborn 'til the end."

"Thank God," Ron said. "I was down to my last nickel when I hit my second one near Lubbock, five years later. Lotta money out the door.

"Lotta booze under the bridge," Joanna added.

"So you don't drink now?" Dango asked.

"Not a drop," he said. "Six months after I met Miss Joanna here, I quit."

"I told him if he didn't quit it was AMF-YOYO," she piped in.

"What's that?" I said.

"Adios motherfucker, you're on your own."

Ron laughed. Dango and I laughed too – sort of. We were both kind of stunned by the language. You would never hear our parents talking this way.

"Couldn't have that," he said. "So I went cold turkey. Haven't had a drop since. She straightened out my finances and she straightened me out."

"I straightened you out alright," she said.

They both chuckled at that comment, which seemed to be about more than just drinking or money.

"Joanna insisted I invest my money in something a little more secure than wildcatting," Ron continued. "So, I always loved motorcycles. Had a Triumph and a Harley. I became partner in a small motorcycle dealership in Dallas. Couldn't own it outright, of course, cause of my record."

"I'm gonna get a Triumph next year," Dango said.

That was news to me. I did know he loved motorcycles. I didn't know he planned to buy one. Come to think of it, he probably just decided on it at that moment. It made sense. Motorcycles went fast and were dangerous. Perfect for Dango.

"So, can you get him a deal?" I asked Ron.

"Nah," Ron replied. "I sold my interest back to the guy. Couldn't stand working with a partner, 'specially him. I knew he'd end up cheating me. Then I'd have to kill him."

Whoa – there it was again. We're driving along having a perfectly enjoyable conversation and then suddenly Ron drops a bomb that lets you know you're driving with an ex-convict. All said with a smile, of course.

"So what do you do now?" I asked, moving on.

"There was a guy came to the dealership selling those little Japanese bikes," Ron said. "Hondas. Ever heard of 'em?"

Dango and I both said, "No."

"Yeah, well they're all the rage in Japan now. Pretty well-made, inexpensive and they're starting to import a shitload of 'em into the States."

"So you're selling those?" I said.

"Nope, better," he went on. "This sales rep knew a guy in LA that assembled the bikes when they came in from Japan. Had a small shop in Compton down by the LA docks with a few Mexican workers. He wanted to sell, so I bought it all, lock, stock and barrel."

"I thought they made them in Japan," I said.

"Yeah they do. But they're shipped over here in boxes on freighters. I pick up the boxes, assemble them, and then truck them to dealers in the Western U.S."

"So, you think Japanese motorcycles will catch on?" Dango asked.

"Joanna thinks so," Ron said. "And that's good enough for me."

"The Japs are real smart," Joanna added. "The bikes are inexpensive, well-made and they're starting to advertise."

I have no idea what kind of car Ron drives today – or if he's still alive. I just remember thinking about Ron and Joanna often in the 20 years after 1961. Just an ex-con and a busty bookkeeper, no business degrees, no higher education, but if they stuck with what they were doing, they're still rich to this day. Very rich. We discovered as the ride went on that they had other businesses, too. They were creating their own "American Dream" far from the American dreams of Shaker and Cleveland Heights.

All of this exposition had come in the first hour or so of a five-hour drive. By now, the big Cadillac had reached the Oklahoma line. Route 66 continued and the landscape looked exactly as it had after leaving Amarillo – flat and boring. When we reached the small town of Elk City, Oklahoma, Ron pulled off at the first gas station restaurant we came to.

"Come on, boys," Ron said. "You look hungry. I'm buying."

After filling the Eldorado (it took 20 gallons of Premium for 11 bucks), we entered the coffee shop and sat down in a shiny new vinyl booth, Dango and I on one side, Joanna and Ron across from us. I started going over in my mind how much mileage we were covering. We were making good time with these first two trips on Thursday. I figured we'd get into Tulsa about 6:30 or 7:00 p.m. and if we could pick up a night ride, with luck we could get to Cleveland on Saturday. That sounded good to me, because it meant I wouldn't have to call my parents again. Dango and I both ordered burgers, fries and chocolate milk shakes. A decent breakfast, a real lunch and luxurious travel in a brand new Cadillac. Hitchhiking was the only way to go.

Once everyone got their food, I opened the conversation again and put my foot in my mouth.

"So, how long have you guys been married?"

Ron and Joanna came out with a little chuckle again and Ron said, "What makes you think we're married?"

"You're not?" Dango said.

"Common law maybe," Joanna laughingly said.

"Listen," Ron started, and then proceeded to talk for the rest of the lunch about the Ron Shank's philosophy of business, relationships and living in America.

I suppose I could try to put it down word-for-word the way I remember it, but it would end up being my words and it's not like it was brilliant, or consistent or even coherent. What it was – was different. Like nothing I've ever heard before or since and in a strange way it made sense. Certainly for Ron.

It all stemmed, I guess, from getting the bulk of your education in prison.

"I do everything by handshake," was the way Ron put it. That was it in a nutshell and Ron applied that to everything. He didn't want anything in writing. If he couldn't count on you with a handshake he certainly couldn't count on you with any written agreement. He tried to deal in cash as often as he could. He let Dango and me know that he really hated the government and didn't want them knowing anything about what he was doing. Same with lawyers. As for Joanna, she was bound by no marriage contract. They had shaken hands on their partnership and he had sealed the deal when he stopped drinking. They were both free in Ron's mind. Freedom and honesty were the two keys to Ron's philosophy and, to him, that's what the handshake symbolized.

If you were honest with the people you met and fulfilled any and all obligations that you agreed to with them, you were free at any time to walk away. Dango and I were mesmerized. I remember thinking at the time that this must have been the philosophy of the old West, the cowboys.

Before we left the restaurant Ron and Joanna went to the bathrooms. Dango turned to me.

"Joanna was playing footsy with me under the table all during lunch," he said. "You think that's what Ron meant about freedom?"

Heading back to the car after lunch, Ron turned to me, "Okay Lee, you want to take it for a while?"

"Sure," I said.

"I'll sit next to you just to make sure you've got the hang of it."

"Should be nothing to it," I offered. "Wouldn't you rather sit in back with Joanna and get a little nap?"

I was pushing for that for obvious reasons, but Ron would have none of it. Probably that prison trust thing: "I'll trust you to drive my car, but only if I'm sitting next to you." He should have been more worried about the trust going on in the back seat.

Everyone got back in the Eldorado and the only change in seating arrangements was my swap with Ron. I pulled back onto 66, gave the big Caddie a little gas and we were back cruising at 70 mph in no time. Compared to the Pontiac the ride was like floating on a cloud. And I'm talking about the Star Chief before I drove it off a cliff.

I think I was the one that started the conversation again. Anything to put off what I was sure was going to happen in the back seat if Ron went to sleep.

"So, how come you guys are going to Tulsa?" I said.

"Good question, Lee," Joanna chimed in. "Come on Ron, let's tell the boys the answer!"

Ron just laughed. Not even Joanna could fluster him by urging him to answer a question which for many people might be embarrassing.

"Well, I'll tell ya," Ron started. "Besides investing in motorcycles after wildcatting, I put a little money in another good, growing business."

"What was that?" Dango bit.

"Porn."

"Porn?!" Dango and I repeated. I recall Dango and I doing that a lot on this leg of the trip: Sitting there with our mouth open, wondering what to say next.

"You mean you make pornographic books and movies?" I asked, trying to figure out how to continue this conversation and keep it somewhat safe.

"Oh no," Ron went on. "I don't produce the stuff, just sell it. I opened a few small pornographic bookstores in this neck of the woods, 'bout the same time I went in on the dealership in Dallas. Noticed there were a lot of lonely men on the ranches and oil fields around here that needed some good reading material. Did real well, too. Probably better than the dealership."

"Almost exactly the same profit," said Joanna the bookkeeper.

"So, you have a bookstore in Tulsa?" Dango asked.

"Yup. But we're headin' up there to close it," Ron said.

"Why?" I asked. "If they're doing so well."

Ron chuckled again.

"Easy answer," Ron said. "Porn bookstores are a cash only, hands-on business. Can't be running bookstores here from Los Angeles. So I opened four new ones in the LA area, shut down the ones I owned in Texas and Oklahoma."

"You mean you have to be in the stores all the time?" Dango said.

"Not all the time, but I've got to go to 'em at least once a week to check the inventory, pick up the cash and make sure my store manager's not skimming."

"Skimming?" I asked.

"Taking money off the profits," Joanna said.

"I used to make the Dallas-Oklahoma City-Tulsa drive once every week when I lived here," Ron said, while yawning at the same time. "Never did it on the same schedule ever. Makes me tired just thinking of it."

"Nobody ever stole from you?" I said.

"Nope, thanks to a prison background and this." Ron opened the glove compartment.

I'm not sure Dango could see in there from the backseat, or even if he was watching, but I saw it big as life – a pearl-handled, shiny Colt 45. Ron closed the glove compartment quickly, leaned back in the corner of where the front seat met the front door and stretched out his legs.

"You're doing fine, Lee," he said. "I can hardly keep my eyes open. Wake me before Tulsa."

"Think we'll catch a few zzzs back here too, honey," said Joanna as she leaned back in her corner.

Ron didn't even acknowledge her. I glanced over at him and he looked like he was already asleep. In the rearview mirror, I could see all of Joanna's expansive sweater as it floated along with the ride of the car. I couldn't see Dango. I didn't want to see Dango. I just prayed he stayed on his side of the backseat. I decided the best course of action was just to keep my eyes forward, focused on this straight Oklahoma section of 66. What I didn't see couldn't hurt me. I turned on the radio and the only station I could get was an Oklahoma City country/western. First song was Patsy Cline's *I Fall to Pieces*. I thought of Ron driving these highways, all times of night or day, listening to this kind of music, and I have to admit it didn't seem all bad. Not exactly the life I would sketch out for myself, but Ron Shanks, ex-con, wildcatter, porno bookstore owner, gun-toting entrepreneur, softly snoring besides me, had some kind of original, only-in-America life. I came to the surprising realization that I liked him, maybe even admired him.

In just two hours of driving and talking, I had been exposed to prison life, wildcatting, motorcycle sales and assembly, the pornography business, open relationships and a philosophy of absolute honesty.

After almost being kicked out of school for a "fuck you all" acrostic, I think I had finally met my philosopher. I heard a little noise from the backseat and took another peek in the rearview mirror.

At first, I couldn't see Joanna. I sat up in the seat and then saw she was now laying down in the backseat with her head on Dango's lap. I shifted my gaze in the mirror to see Dango's face. He looked at me with big open eyes and raised eyebrows, then tilted his head. I'd seen the look before: it was, "What can I do?" Before I went back to concentrating on the road, I glanced over at Ron. He was sleeping like a baby.

The situation that was unfolding was way beyond my experience to handle. I kept my eyes glued to the road, but my mind was racing way over the speed limit. I was sitting next to a sleeping ex-con who had once killed somebody and there was a gun in the glove compartment. In the back seat, my best friend was having some kind of sex with this man's "common law" wife and bookkeeper. What were my options? I could stop, pull over to the side of the road, get out and run. I could wake Ron and see what he wanted to do. Maybe he wouldn't be upset and would just watch. Maybe that's how he and Joanna got their kicks. Or maybe he'd shoot Dango and let me continue driving. Or I could pray that Joanna knew Ron slept like a log and that it would take a head-on collision to wake him; and that's why she felt comfortable enough to take advantage of her strapping young seatmate. It didn't take me long to figure the last option was the only viable one.

The next 15 to 20 minutes were the longest minutes I've ever spent driving. I drove like a saint. Never broke the speed limit. (I could just imagine a cop pulling us over.) Never let myself get in a situation where I had to brake hard. Kept the radio low playing those sad ballads and love songs. Fortunately we were in Oklahoma, so there were no sharp curves or turns. Route 66 just proceeded in a straight line and the Eldorado glided over it like a mattress on wheels.

It was when we started to enter Oklahoma City and the traffic increased that I began to sweat. Literally. I had to stop at a few lights and follow the signs to the Turner Turnpike for the last leg to Tulsa.

The break in the rhythm of the drive had me worried and I kept stealing looks over at Ron. He never once opened his eyes. When I stopped at the entrance booth to pick up my ticket for the turnpike, I took my first turn-around look to the backseat. Dango and Joanna had retreated to their separate corners, legs extended, heads back, eyes closed. They were sleeping or faking, I didn't care which. All I knew was the crisis had been avoided. My careful driving had saved my friend and I would make sure he knew it once we got back to Cleveland. I put the turnpike ticket on the seat between me and the sleeping Ron and accelerated on to the brand new four-lane highway toward Tulsa, only a little over 100 miles ahead.

For some reason Oklahoma in 1961 had two of the finest, newest highways in the United States: the Turner Turnpike went from Oklahoma City to Tulsa and the Will Rogers Turnpike ran from Tulsa to the Missouri state line. They were absolutely beautiful new four-lane expressways, and thank God they were, because the landscape was even more boring than the flatlands of Texas. It was almost as if Oklahomans had built the turnpikes as a favor to drivers so you could pass through their state as quickly as possible. Once the Eldorado hit that fresh smooth pavement, it seemed to just naturally want to go about 80 mph. I had to watch it, keep the speed about 70 mph, sit back, enjoy the ride and take care of my sleeping fellow passengers.

I must admit it seemed a little odd to be driving a car full of sleeping travelers. The last time I'd been driving alone with a sleeper, I'd launched the Star Chief off the road on the way up to Sequoia. I wonder how anxious Ron would have been to hand over the wheel of his prized Eldorado if I'd told him that tale. It felt good driving again after the accident. I was now keenly aware of staying alert while driving. If I sensed myself tiring, I would immediately open the windows, squeeze the steering wheel tightly and stop as soon as I could. I would not drive and drink beer again. What surprised me was that people would pick up hitchhikers and actually let them drive their cars. As it turned out, Ron was only the first driver on the trip to let Dango and me take the wheel.

On the way toward Tulsa, in the quiet Cadillac, I began thinking, not surprisingly after what had just happened in the back seat, about sex. And I'm not talking about the way I usually thought about sex at 18, imagining Brigitte Bardot writhing around in the backseat telling me to pull off the road and help her pull off her too-tight skirt. I actually remember thinking about it like a grown up might think about it.

Why did people react to sex differently? Why did some of my friends have sex and talk about it? Why did some remain silent on the subject? Why had Dango taken such a chance with Joanna? What would I have done in his position?

I had always thought, to that moment, that Dango and I were somewhat similar in our feelings about sex. I knew, though, that I would never have let Joanna seduce me in the back seat of the Cadillac. I would have been scared to death. Besides that, even though she probably had "twin 44s" of her own, she was a little old for me. I didn't find her all that attractive. Then, I had to stop and think about that: since when did an 18-year-old have to find somebody attractive to have sex with them? Jesus, I began to realize, I was the prude in the Eldorado. I knew then that I actually equated love with sex. At least, a little love. Even in the early '60s, that was a little too prim and proper. Where had I gone wrong?

Dango and I actually had our first encounter with "sex" back in Roxboro Junior High. One of the girls in our seventh grade class had taken a liking to me and, instead of talking to me, she made arrangements with Dango for herself and another girl to get together with us at her house after school and play "doctor." It turned into a silly "show and touch" session with all four of us having no knowledge of what we were seeing or touching. There were no hygiene courses in the '60s, until the first year in high school. By ninth grade, which was the last year of junior high, Dango and I would be walking girls home from school and "making out." There were Friday night dances at the local YMCA that our parents drove us to. In classic baseball/sex terminology, the farthest anyone got, that I knew in junior high, was "second base."

By high school, everything changed. Sex and beer became the two primary weekend preoccupations. As I've already mentioned, beer was a lot easier to get. Only a few of the guys at University School had steady dates through high school. Neither Dango nor I were one of the few. I think we double-dated a couple of times with Laurel and Hathaway Brown girls, but those dates never got serious. If you had a shot at some "heavy action" with a private school girl, you went out alone. Your car became the "playing field." My favorite "parking" memories took place in winter. I'd leave the Star Chief running, heat on, a six-pack outside in the snow, windows steaming as I talked and clawed my way to "third base." Never further with a Laurel or Hathaway Brown girl.

Lehmann, always the brilliant one, never wasted his time dating private school girls. He did his fishing at Orange High School near where he lived in Pepper Pike. He swore by it. He never told any tales, but Dango and I just knew that he was "scoring." One night, in our junior year, Lehmann got Dango and me dates with Orange girls. Nothing was ever really stated, but Lehmann let us know that these girls went "all the way" on dates. I don't remember the first part of the evening. I do know we didn't go to any parties where we'd run into Laurel or Hathaway Brown girls. We ended up back at my house. My parents were in New York for the weekend and therefore Lehmann, Dango and I each had private rooms. What happened with the other guys, I'm not sure. According to them, they scored. What happened to me, I still shake my head about.

Sarah, my date, was lovely – long jet-black hair, a willowy body and sharp facial features. We hit it off all night and when we got back to our "private" room, I thought nothing was going to stop the passion. I could tell she wasn't a virgin and in a few more minutes, I wouldn't be either. Then, just as I was "rounding third headed for 'home'," she put on the brakes.

"I can't do this with you," she said panting.

"What?" I gasped.

"I can't go all the way with you."

"Why not?"

I was still working as hard as I could to break down this sudden reticence. She grabbed and held both my hands, then looked me in the eyes. "You're really nice," she said. "I like you too much. I want to go out with you again."

I was speechless. All I wanted to do was shout, "No, I'm not nice. I'm an asshole. I just want to get laid." But that didn't seem like a winning argument. So, I spent the next half hour trying to explain that the "nice" thing to do would be to put the "nice boy" out of his misery. Didn't work and I couldn't, or wouldn't, force it.

In the summer of 1960, I visited my first and only whorehouse. I tell the story here because I could never relate the true story back then – all my peers would have laughed at me.

It was a summer Friday night, and all of my closest friends had dates or other plans. It looked like, horror of horrors, I might have to spend the evening at home, when Scott Kelly, a classmate from University School called and asked if I wanted to go with him and two other guys to a "whorehouse in Canton." The minute I heard it, I thought to myself this was probably going to be a wild goose chase, but "what the heck", anything was better than staying at home with my parents. For some reason, we took two cars. I think Scott, the leader of this expedition, thought it would be better if we didn't all show up at the same time.

I was paired-up with another classmate I knew only slightly, named Richie. Scott paired us up by who looked oldest. Richie had freckles and sandy-colored hair, so the two of us went in his car because we, by far, looked the youngest. We had the ubiquitous six-pack of beer to share on the ride and followed Scott in his souped-up '56 Chevy toward Canton.

Richie and I hit it off, laughing for most of the trip at the absurdity of driving to Canton for a whorehouse when we lived in Cleveland.

The draw, according to Scott, was that these were going to be "hot white whores." Scott had the address and directions and led us to a suburb of Canton packed with new tract houses. In the middle of one block he signaled for us to pull over. We stopped behind his car and cut the lights following his lead. He came back to our driver's side window. Richie rolled it down.

"The house is up there on the next block," he said, motioning to the street that ran perpendicular to the one where we were parked.

"We'll go in first," he continued. "Wait for us here."

He went back to his Chevy. Richie rolled the window back up. We looked at each other and cracked up.

"This is a joke," Richie said.

"Got to be," I answered. "Does this look like a neighborhood where there'd be a whorehouse?"

We watched as Scott turned his lights back on and turned onto the next street. He went down about three houses and then turned into the driveway of the fourth house. The house was completely dark. Richie and I were still laughing.

We stopped laughing when we saw a man with a large flashlight exit the front door of the house and walk up to the car. The headlights on the Chevy went off and the man leaned down to Scott's window. He held the light on Scott and his seat mate as he talked to them. Richie and I, from about 150 yards away, watched the action dumbfounded. I remember thinking to myself, "My God, it must be the real thing." I also remember looking around the neighborhood, wondering if anyone else lived there. All the houses looked dark for 10:00 p.m. on a Friday night.

After about three minutes, the man turned and walked back to the house. Scott turned on his lights again and backed out of the driveway. The man paused to watch him leave, then re-entered the house. Scott drove off, apparently to go around the block and pull up behind us. He came back to the driver's window on Richie's car.

"What happened?" Richie said when he rolled down the window again.

"He thought we were too young," Scott said. "We didn't have any ID."

"Fat chance, we'll get in," I said.

"Well, you're here," Scott said. "Might as well give it a try. We'll wait here,"

He headed back to his car. Richie and I looked at each other.

"You drive," Richie said. "You look older."

Of all the kids in University School in our class, Richie was probably the only one that could have said that and have it be true. With the freckles and light skin, he looked like a 14-year-old Howdy Doody.

"Okay," I said.

We got out of our seats, opened both doors and passed each other as we walked behind the car to switch seats. When I got back in the driver's seat, I started the car, turned on the lights and put it in gear.

"Here goes nothing," I said as we started off. I figured, as we drove that short distance, that if Scott couldn't get in because he looked too young, no way the two "baby faces" in this car were going to make it. Maybe that certainty we were going to fail gave me the bravado to perform completely against my nature in the next few minutes.

I pulled into the driveway of the fourth house and stopped. The guy came out with the flashlight and I gulped a bit. He was big, about 6'2", wore an old Cleveland Indians cap and had a face that looked like it had been punched-in a few times. He also wore a flannel long-sleeve shirt, unbuttoned over a white T-shirt. Way too warmly dressed for the middle of summer in Ohio. He talked quickly and to the point as he shone the light in our faces.

"What do you want?"

Maybe it was from hanging out with Dango so much, or maybe it was because I didn't think any of this was real, but some other character besides Lee answered him in a low, tough voice, "What the hell do you think we want?"

"Where are you from?" he asked.

"Just drove up from State," I answered.

To this day, I have no idea where that answer came from. At that time, I had never even been to Ohio State University or ever set foot in Columbus.

He put the light on my face.

"How old are you?"

"20," I answered immediately.

He put the light on Richie's freckled face.

"You got some ID?"

"Sure thing," Richie answered as he took out his wallet and passed him a Maine driver's license.

The guy looked at it and passed it back.

"Okay. Cut the lights, take it around back and park in the garage."

He started back to the front door. At that instance, my hands and knees started shaking. Baby-faced Richie had an ID! Who would have thought that? This was actually going to happen. I could barely drive the car down the 20 feet of the driveway and pull it into the attached garage. There was another man waiting for us at the door from the garage into the house.

Richie and I followed this man into the small kitchen where there was a chrome and Formica table. On the table there was a cash box. I assumed that was the man's office, where he took care of the business. He kind of looked like a bookkeeper, small and mousy, nothing like the truck driver at the front door; also in the room was a woman, in a light purple robe. She looked a little like Donna Reed. The man turned to us, and in keeping with the no-nonsense tone of the evening, said, "Who's first?"

Not giving Richie a chance to talk, I answered for both of us.

"He is," I said, barely able to get it out.

"Okay," Mousy said. "You wait in front."

I was out of the kitchen in a flash and didn't look back. I walked the short hallway to the living room where the big guy with the flashlight and another older guy in a gray suit and white shirt without a tie were watching television. They motioned for me to sit down on the couch across from the TV. I sat down without saying a word. No one spoke. The only furniture in the room was the console TV on a small table, the couch with a blanket thrown across the back and two straight-back chairs the guys were sitting on. All the windows had the shades closed.

I don't know what I expected a whorehouse to look like, but this certainly wasn't it. I'd seen Westerns with whorehouses populated with big, friendly, buxom beauties and madams that looked like Mae West. They always had a piano player with a full whisky glass next to the keys. Nothing had prepared me for a brothel in a '50s tract house without any furniture in a suburb of Canton, Ohio. It was cold, scary and anything but sexy. The only thing that seemed somewhat appropriate was the TV show the guys in front were watching – *The Untouchables*. Sitting in a whorehouse watching Robert Stack running around killing a bunch of mobsters from the twenties would have made me laugh if I hadn't been scared to death.

After what seemed like an hour, but I'm sure was only 10 minutes, the mousy bookkeeper came in and delivered one of the all-time great one liners to me: "Okay, you're up."

I was anything but "up," but I did stand up and follow him back into the kitchen. We passed Richie in the hall heading to the depressing living room to take his turn watching *The Untouchables*. The bookkeeper delivered me to the Donna Reed look-alike, who, on closer examination was nowhere near as pretty as Donna, and she took me back to the bedroom. We entered and she closed the door behind us. It dawned on me at that moment that she was the hooker. My virginity was going to be lost to a middle-aged Canton, Ohio housewife, free-lancing for an extra 50 bucks. Any teenage ardor that might have lingered, after sitting in an empty suburban tract house living room with gangsters watching gangsters, left my body instantly. But I was committed now, so I kept playing my part.

She opened our short dialogue: "So what do you want?"

I tried to respond, but found I had no voice. All I could get out was one word. "Fuck," I squeaked.

What transpired in the next 10 minutes can best be described as a farce. Which means it's best not described at all. Let's just say Brigitte Bardot, Marylyn Monroe and any other sex goddess I ever fantasized about, working together, could not have aroused my sleeping manhood. The Canton housewife gave it a good try, but after the allotted time gave up her efforts.

She smiled at me as she was putting back on her robe and I was hurriedly putting back on my pants.

"You be sure to come back when you're a little older," she said kindly.

I don't remember a thing about getting out of that house, but I know it was fast. Next thing I remember, we had hooked up with the other guys and stopped at a Royal Castle to share a 12-pack of their miniature burgers. I remember Scott asking me a question.

"So how was it?"

I looked him straight in the eye, and with a slight knowing smile and a deep voice said: "Great."

So much for honesty about sex in the early '60s. By the time I was driving Ron's Eldorado to Tulsa, I imagined myself an experienced lover with three notches on my belt: A one night fling with a girl dubbed a "nymphomaniac" from Orange High School; an afternoon with the first girl I "loved" from Cleveland Heights High School during my senior year (she later dumped me, my first "heartbreak," because she was just using me while her real boyfriend was away at college); and then, of course, Barbara from Long Beach.

Neither Dango nor I were prepared for the revolutionary changes in sexual mores that waited for us up ahead in the later '60s. I often wonder if any of us were.

"How ya doing, Lee?" Ron said from the front passenger seat.

"Sleep well?" I said.

"Always do," he replied.

"Only about 15 more miles to Tulsa," I said. "This car sure is easy to drive."

He looked in the backseat. Dango and Joanna were still sound asleep in their respective corners.

"I bought this Caddie with some of the profits I made from my greatest porno book deal ever," he said, turning back to the front.

Another story from Ron was on the way, I thought. Then I thought, "I wonder how many of his stories I will never hear."

CHAPTER 7

Tulsa to St. Louis

Ron had me pull over after we exited the Turner Turnpike. He took the wheel. The two sleepers in back awoke.

"I'll drive you right to the entrance of the Will Rogers," he said as he pulled back into traffic.

It didn't take long to get to the entrance of the next turnpike. Ron knew the way and Tulsa wasn't very big. There was another wide expanse of road before the Will Rogers toll booths, and a large shoulder area to the right where Ron guided the Eldorado and stopped. He was the first one to pop out of the car and head back to unlock the trunk. His hour nap had obviously recharged his batteries and he was ready to go attend to the closing of his last porn bookstore in Oklahoma. Dango and I got out a little slower and went back to the trunk to claim our bags. Joanna got out last and gave each of us a farewell hug. I've got to admit, it was like hugging someone with a couple of small throw pillows under their shirt. Dango's hug was a little longer than mine.

Ron slapped each of us on the back and shook our hand. "Thanks a bunch, you guys," he said. "Have a great trip. You've got a couple of hours 'til dark. Catch a good one."

He headed back to the driver's seat. "C'mon Joanna, let's hit it."

Joanna jumped in the front passenger seat without even another glance at us. Ron started the car, looked out his side window and when he saw a break, floored the big Eldorado, made an illegal U-turn and headed back into Tulsa. That quickly, they were gone.

Dango and I stood looking at each other as we had at the start of the ride. I think I must have shaken my head in disbelief at what a bizarre experience we'd just had, because Dango thought I was shaking my head at him.

"Lee," he said. "What could I do?"

"Bob," I replied. "Maybe a 'no' would have been in order."

"I did that," he said. "She wanted to do the deed – all the way."

"Oh, so you just settled on part way?" I said. "Do you know he had a fucking gun in the glove compartment? We're lucky we're not road kill somewhere on the Oklahoma prairie."

"Jesus, he had a gun?" Dango gulped.

"Sure did."

"I tried not to," he went on. "But do you know what she said to me, when I said 'no'?"

"Of course not."

"She like blew softly and whispered into my ear at the same time and said, 'No one's ever complained about my blow jobs.'"

I couldn't help but break out laughing. "She actually said that?"

"Swear to God. So what could I do? I couldn't hurt her feelings."

"Well, someday, you're gonna repay me for driving like a nun while you were getting head in the backseat, while her boyfriend, husband, ex-con, killer was asleep in the front."

We were laughing so hard, we hadn't even noticed a car had pulled up behind us on the shoulder. It was a shout that made us turn around.

"You guys are having so much fun, I guess you're not looking for a ride."

I'll be damned if it wasn't another '57 Chevy Bel Air, 'cept this one was a cherry, red-and-white, four-door hard top. A young man – looked to be in his 20s – was standing by the open driver's door smiling at us.

"We would love a ride," Dango shouted back.

"Well, come on," he said. "But tell me you got licenses. I got to get all the way to St. Louis by tomorrow morning and no way I can drive all night."

"We got licenses," I answered.

"We're good drivers," Dango added.

We each picked up our bags and went to meet him at the trunk of the Chevy. I could hardly wait to look at my map. We had started this day in New Mexico, had already crossed a good chunk of Texas and Oklahoma and we were going to be through almost all of Missouri by morning. Two '57 Chevys and a '60 Cadillac Eldorado - why would anyone ever take a Greyhound?

This time I grabbed the backseat and let Dango ride shotgun. After driving the last leg with Ron and Joanna into Tulsa, I was a little tired and figured I could use some rest. Once we were settled, our new driver pulled out right away. He picked up his ticket at the tollbooth and in minutes we were rolling along at 70, headed northeast on another beautiful Oklahoma turnpike.

"My name's Charles Bennett," our driver said. "But you can call me Chuck."

Dango and I introduced ourselves and went through the whole Dango nickname explanation, how we got here, why we were going back to Cleveland, how old we were, etc, etc. Chuck gave us a little of his story.

"I'm a St. Louis boy, born and bred," he said. "Been a Cardinals fan since before I could read. Which was a little late," he continued and chuckled. "Which probably explains why I skipped college and joined the army."

I had already guessed the army part – there was a set of dress khakis with sergeant stripes hanging on the hook above the driver's side back door.

"You're already a sergeant?" I said.

"Hey, I've been in three years," he said. "Did my basic at Fort Leonard Wood, spent two years over in Germany, now I'm finishing up down at Fort Hood in Texas. I'm the best E-5 clerk the army's ever seen. You should see me type."

"What's E-5?" Dango asked.

"That's your army pay grade," Chuck said. "If you're not an E-5 after three years you're either a moron or dead."

He said that with a chuckle too. It kind-of sums up the Chuck Bennett we came to know on this nighttime ride. Always a smile, didn't take himself seriously and never got angry even when we gave him every reason to.

Chuck and Dango soon were chatting away as the '57 Bel Air sped along the new turnpike. I listened for a while, enough time to learn there were three important things in Chuck's life: His girlfriend, who he was headed to St. Louis to see; his '57 Chevy, which he had bought from his Dad when he returned from Germany a year ago; and the city of St. Louis itself. He loved everything about it, especially the Cardinals and Stan Musial, and Red Schoendienst.

"Karen and I are getting married next spring," I heard Chuck tell Dango. "Just as soon as I get out of the army."

"Boy, that's great," Dango replied. "How old are you?"

I loved the way Dango always cut right to the point. I'd been thinking the same thing: "Wasn't this guy a little young to be getting married?"

"Just turned 23," Chuck said. "Karen's 22. We dated all through high school. She stayed true to me for the two years I was in Germany. I'm just lucky, I guess. I've always known she was the one for me."

"You are lucky," Dango agreed.

I knew he was thinking exactly what I was thinking, "No way I'm getting married that early. I've got a lot of fooling around to do." Little did either one of us know we'd both be married by 24.

"How do you like the seats?" Chuck asked.

When neither of us answered he went on, "The car seats," Chuck said. "That's real leather, not Vinyl. Drove down to Mexico one weekend and had 'em put in."

I had noticed the black tuck-and-roll seats. They were pretty fancy for the Chevy and definitely not original with a red-and-white color scheme. I leaned down to smell them and I've got to admit the smell of the genuine leather was kind of nice. I almost stayed down there with my head on the seat because I was beginning to feel very tired, but then I forced myself to get up to check a couple of things. First I took the map out of my left rear pocket to see if we were doing as well as I thought we were. Dango and Chuck kept talking while I calculated. We had covered well over 500 miles since we'd left Clovis that morning. When we reached St. Louis, we'd have added on another 400. Cleveland was only about 500 miles from St. Louis. It was now about 7:30 Thursday evening. I figured, with an early start out of St. Louis and some luck, we could be in Cleveland Friday night. Saturday arrival should be a cinch. I did notice, however, that it was already starting to get dark, so I asked Chuck the other thing I wanted to check. "Hey Chuck, what time is it?"

He looked at the watch on his left wrist on the steering wheel. He must have bought it in Germany, because that thing was bigger than a half dollar and had more numbers and circles than I'd ever seen on a watch.

"Exactly 8:44," he said.

"Thanks," I replied.

I opened up the map a little more, and sure enough, there were the little red-and-yellow dotted lines showing the time zones starting up in Canada and running down and through the states. We'd lost an hour almost as soon as we left Clovis and entered Texas.

Switched from Mountain Daylight to Central Daylight.

"Listen, Lee," Chuck said. "Since you're in back, why don't you get a little shut eye and rest up. You can take the first leg when I get tired."

"Dango, you want to take the first shift?" I said, trying to throw it back to him since I'd already been driving a couple of hours.

"Maybe," Dango said. "But you go ahead and get some sleep. I'll see how I feel when Chuck stops."

"We'll stop and get something to eat in Joplin, just after we get out of Oklahoma," Chuck added.

"Okay, guys. See you then," I said.

I lay down on the new leather, closed my eyes and smiled. This hitchhiking across country that I had been so apprehensive about had so far been an incredible experience. Once again, Dango had forced me to do something that I was thoroughly enjoying. I began to think ahead to my next year in college, away from Cleveland, and I was now actually looking forward to it. New experiences, new adventures would be good, I thought.

That realization I had just before falling asleep was a big step for me. Up until that moment, 1961 had hit me pretty hard. Almost getting kicked out of University School to start the year was just the beginning. Shortly after that, in March, my dad suffered his third heart attack. I believe to this day it was due to his lifestyle and Type A personality, but I always have a twinge of guilt that escapade with the acrostic played some part. He recovered, but began to plan his eventual retirement from the company where he was a director. Once mom and dad knew I was never going to attend Princeton, we had to scramble and find a decent college where admissions were still open. The first week of Easter break, I flew to Los Angeles and took a copy of the offensive US Newspaper to the new Claremont Men's College to show them why I was punished. They accepted me, more because they were looking for students from other states to fill out their geographical distributions than because of my academic prowess.

Since I was going to be headed to California to go to school, and since Jay already lived there, my parents started making plans to move out, too. They put our big 2-lot house on Berkshire Road in Cleveland Heights on the market. My dad, after he recovered, began looking for consulting work in either Los Angeles or San Francisco. Probably the main reason I succumbed so quickly to Dango's desire to go back to Cleveland that day on Moro Rock was that I realized 1961 might be the year my family ties to Cleveland were severed for good.

If I had been able to dream and see the future, I would have known in fact that that's exactly what happened. In September my dad stepped down from his position on the board of the Cleveland company and accepted an advisory position with a subsidiary company they had purchased in San Francisco. In November, while I was at school in Claremont, they sold the house on Berkshire Road. In early December they leased a huge apartment on Russian Hill with a view looking out toward the Golden Gate Bridge. By 1962, the only ties the Livingstons had left in Cleveland were a few good friends and the second lot they didn't sell bordering the house on Berkshire Road.

But the vivid dream I did have on that tuck-and-roll leather was much different. Instead of the future, I flashed back to me and Dango on Moro Rock. And instead of my pulling Dango back to safety, we both leapt into the void. We weren't leaping to our deaths; we knew we could fly. And that's what we did. Arms extended, we swooped and soared from Sequoia to Cleveland Heights. Over my brother's flimsy cantilevered house in the Hollywood Hills to skim the Pacific waves breaking on the shore near the power plant at Seal Beach. Floating high above the tacky little desert city of Las Vegas to dive down the sheer concrete face of Hoover Dam, pulling up sharply before we hit the Colorado. We even flew over ourselves as we lay next to the giant turbines, with our shirts off in the open rail car, chugging across the Arizona desert. There was more to the dream, of course, and I don't know how I remember the little I do, because I didn't wake in the middle of it. Maybe I was still partially awake when I dreamed it. Maybe it was just so beautiful that my mind keeps replaying it at other times in my life when I'm happy.

Reality is never as good or as bad as the stuff of dreams. After Dango and I got back to Cleveland in the summer of 1961, we drifted apart a bit. No rift or anything, but we had been together every day for two solid months. We each had other friends to see, other girls to say our farewells to, and different things to get in order before we left for college. We saw each other at a few parties and at the last beer bust of the summer by the Chagrin River, but there was no tearful, hugging best friend farewell. Not that Dango and I would have ever done that anyway, and we had already made tentative plans for the next summer. We didn't think anything was over.

Dango needed money when we got back to Cleveland, so he signed on to work with a '59 University School graduate who ran his own tree service. In the '60s many of the magnificent elm trees throughout Ohio came down with Dutch elm disease. There was no cure, so they had to be cut down. Dan Moore had started his own tree service in the summer of 1960 and, using his high school and college buddies for labor, they undercut the prices charged by larger established nursery services. Dango had worked with him on a few jobs and Moore quickly realized he had special skills. Since he had no fear and loved working hard, he was perfect as a "flyer." The flyer was suspended by ropes and pulleys clipped on to a leather saddle belt and, with nailed shoes on his feet, climbed up to trim the upper branches of the elm before felling the giant tree. Dango would swing in the leather saddle through the treetops, wielding a heavy chainsaw, and cut large branches down with the reckless abandon of some mad Tarzan. He loved it. He was so good at it that Moore, near the end of the summer, to maximize the work, got another truck and let Dango go out on separate jobs with his own crew.

A couple of times I signed on to go with him. It wasn't all that easy working as a day laborer with your best friend as your boss. We didn't get into any fights, but Dango was a taskmaster and nobody worked as hard or enjoyed the work as much as he did. I was strictly ground crew, carried and stacked logs, loaded branches on to the truck and raked up afterwards. Dango made every effort to get two jobs done in a day. A job usually consisted of one elm that had to be taken out.

I'll never forget one job we had on Scarborough Road in Cleveland Heights. Scarborough was a straight street of smaller houses for the Heights, no giant lots, just one home-driveway-hedge next to another home-driveway-hedge all down the block. The diseased elm was in the front yard of one house in the middle of the block and leaned a little towards the house. Dango went up and cut off some of the larger, higher branches, then came down and said, "Let's one-cut it."

On a big elm like this one, which was leaning the wrong way, it would probably have been smarter to "top" it first – take off a large section of the main trunk at the top and lower it with pulleys before doing the main cut at the base. Dango always tried to do "one-cuts" though, cause if you "one-cutted" you could get in and out of the job quicker and make more money. So Dango tied a rope high up on the trunk of the elm and the "ground crew" grabbed the other end of the rope and pulled the tree toward the street and away from the house.

Dango then started the one-cut at the base of the tree, on the side away from the house. As the cut got deeper, we, on the ground crew, kept the tension on the rope to pull it toward us so the elm would fall across the front yard toward the street. When we heard the wood beginning to "rip" as Dango kept the saw cutting, we pulled even harder. Just when the tree began to give, the rope broke. Dango kept cutting and the tree began to sway back and forth toward the house, toward the yard. Dango finished the cut and we all stood helpless and watched as the large elm began to fall wherever it was going to fall. It finally fell toward the cut and away from the house, but not exactly where we had hoped. Instead of falling straight across the front yard to the street, it fell across and through the hedge to the neighbor's adjoining yard. Fortunately, it was a weekday and no one was at home. Dango immediately sprang into action and grabbed his chainsaw to begin cutting the top of the tree in the neighbor's yard into removable pieces. He shouted orders at the same time.

"Come on, guys," he yelled. "Soon as I cut a piece, two of you get it to the truck. Lee, get the broom and rake and clean the sawdust and branches, quick as you can."

At least I was good for something. Cleaning up after Dango was what I did best.

"There can't be any trace this thing fell in the neighbor's yard. Let's do it fast before anyone shows up."

Once Dango had sawed the elm into movable pieces, he pitched in and carried sizable logs to the truck too. In just under an hour, before anyone returned home, we had removed all the evidence that part of a giant elm had fallen into the neighbor's yard. Dango even had a gas-powered blower to blow away the sawdust we couldn't get with a rake or broom. There was only one problem – the beautiful, manicured hedge between the properties. It ran along nice and straight and all of a sudden, smack dab in the middle, there was a huge, semi-circular hole where the elm had fallen. I, of course, pointed it out to him.

"Dango," I said, standing by the hole. "How you gonna fix this?"

He studied it for a while. He actually crossed his arms and rubbed his chin while thinking. Then he turned into a sculptor.

Dango propped up the smashed pieces of the hedge, cut other hedge parts and branches and began to fill the hole. In 15 minutes, from a distance, you couldn't tell there was anything wrong. Of course, in a few days, all the new hedge construction would turn brown and the owners would scream. But by then Dango would have been paid. Dango stepped back and looked at his handiwork.

He turned to the rest of us with a smile.

The next line was especially for me:

"In 20 years will it make a difference?" he said. Everyone laughed. I laughed a little less than the other guys. I'd heard it before.

"Tonight you're mine completely.

You give your love so sweetly.

Tonight the look of love is in your eyes but,

Will you still love me tomorrow?"

I awoke in the backseat of Chuck's '57 Chevy to my favorite song of 1961: The Shirelles' *Will You Still Love Me Tomorrow*. I was smiling as I sat up and stretched. Outside it was dark.

"Hey, good timing," Chuck said. "We just left Oklahoma. 'Bout to stop and get some food."

"What time is it?" I asked.

Dango turned back and smiled at me. "A little after 11," he said.

"Did you sleep any?"

"Maybe a catnap here and there. Chuck and I talked a lot."

I did wonder what the two of them found to talk about, but I didn't wonder about it for long. We were back on Route 66 now cutting through the outskirts of Joplin and the first open restaurant/truck stop Chuck saw, he pulled off. He dropped us by the restaurant.

"I'm going to go fill it up," he said. "I'll be right in."

He drove over to the pumps. I turned to Dango. "He wouldn't just ditch us here, would he?" I said.

Dango slapped me on the back, laughing. "C'mon Lee," he said. "I've been talking to him for close to two hours. He's a sweetheart. He goes to church every Sunday. He wouldn't hurt a fly, or lie to us."

We went into the truck stop's restaurant, Dango still laughing and teasing me for being worried about Chuck. There were about four booths and the same number of tables in a room, just off where they took the money for the gasoline. Along the wall furthest from the cashier there was a counter with 10 stools. Behind the counter was a grill, Coke machine, coffee maker and a couple of blenders. Probably looked like a million other places on highways throughout the United States. Sitting on the stool was a slender black woman I guessed to be in her early 40s, in a starched blue and white waitress uniform. Behind the counter, dressed in white with an apron, stood a large older black man. The only other people in the room were two truckers finishing up their dinner at one of the tables. You could tell they were truckers because they were in uniform. They both wore blue work shirts with the sleeves rolled up over white tee shirts. They both had baseball caps – one was a John Deere, the other a Mack Truck cap with bulldog.

"Sit anywhere," the waitress said. "I'll bring you some water."

Dango and I took a booth by the window. She came over with the water and two plastic covered, single-sheet menus.

"What the hell are you two boys doing in Joplin, Missouri so late at night?" she asked as she put the water and menus down.

I looked up at her, surprised that she had taken such a familiar a tone with two complete strangers. She looked right back at me, straight in the eyes, showing perfect white teeth in a large smile. On her starched shirt was a name pin: "Reola."

"Whoa," I smiled back. "I just woke up. I don't know if I'm ready for the second degree."

"We're hitchhiking to Cleveland," Dango said. "And you better set another place; our ride's eating too."

"Big Lou, you hear that? We got some rich, big city white boys slummin' through Joplin. Better put on the fillet of sole."

"Rich?!" Dango and I said at the same time.

"Sure 'nuff," she went on with a smile. "You can spend your summer hitchhiking around the country, you got money to burn. Where you from – Shaker Heights?"

"Close enough," I laughed. "Cleveland Heights. How'd you know that?"

"I been around," she said. "But here comes your driver, I better get you another set up."

She headed back to the counter as Chuck came over to our booth and sat down. It was about then that I heard the music playing over the speakers. It was Bobby Blue Bland's original version of *Turn on Your Love Light*. Reola came back with a set up and another menu.

"You lived in Cleveland?" I asked.

"Eighty-ninth near Chester for 10 years," she said. "My dad worked for Republic Steel, my mom was a maid in Shaker Heights."

Eighty-ninth and Chester was part of that large black area between the Heights and downtown Cleveland that whites only passed through.

"How'd you end up here?" I asked.

"That's a long story," she said. "If I were you guys, I'd order up the special there. And if I feel like it, I'll fill you in a little when I come back."

The "special", paper-clipped to the menu, was a bacon cheeseburger, fries and a large Coke for $2.75.

"Sounds good to me," Chuck said. "I'm starving. You guys want to make it three?"

Dango and I agreed, although it sounded like a little more than I wanted at almost 11:30 p.m. Maybe Chuck would be treating.

Reola went back to the counter, gave Lou our order, took care of the bill with the two truckers and shared a laugh with them about something. After that, she brought the Cokes back to our booth. Another Bobby Blue Bland song, *Further on up the Road*, came out over the speaker.

Dango recognized it: "That's no jukebox. You playing an album?"

"You know Bobby Bland?" she asked.

"Sure," Dango answered. "You ever been to Gleason's?"

"You not going to tell me you 'Heights' boys go to Gleason's."

"As often as we can," I said.

"Well you should enjoy the music. That's a tape Big Lou and I put together for ourselves during the late shift. No black R&B stations in Joplin."

She went to get our burgers and fries. After she served us, she took a chair from a nearby table, flipped it around so the back of the chair faced us, sat down, put her elbows up on the back and let us have it.

"You know how I knew you was from the Heights?" she said – not waiting for or expecting an answer. "Way you walked in here. Once I heard you was going to Cleveland, I said to myself – Heights boys. Hell, my mamma had two boys like you. I had two boys like you, too. You walked in here nice and comfortable, like you owned the place. Most people come into a strange burger joint in Joplin, Missouri after 11 at night might be a little 'trepidacious.' A little uneasy. Not you guys – you ain't got enough sense for that. That's because it's your right to go anywhere, do anything. That's your upbringing – you're Heights boys."

I'd managed to eat about half my bacon cheeseburger, which was great by the way, before I was able to protest, "That's not necessarily true. And what do you mean you and your mom had boys like us?"

"Course it's true. You boys even been to Gleason's, for God's sake. Your parents wouldn't do that. You been taught you can do anything. You've been given most everything and you're not old enough to know any better. I know what I'm talking 'bout, cause my mamma was a maid for the Butlers up on Sherbourne Road in Shaker Heights. She helped raise their two boys during the war. And then, after we moved to Detroit. I started as a maid in the '50s for a family in Grosse Point. Helped raise two white boys of my own. Probably your age now."

I choked a little swallowing one of my French fries. Maybe she did know a little of what she was talking about. I remembered the black maid, Jessie, that Jay and I had when I was in elementary school. Every day after school, I'd come home to Jessie and she'd fix me a snack, watch TV with me and play games with me. She did everything. I loved Jessie.

"I didn't have a maid," Dango piped in.

"Neither did I," said Chuck, not to be left out.

"You around it, you pick it up," said Reola back to Dango.

"Okay, Miss Knows It All," I said to keep up the sparring. "You still haven't told us why you left Cleveland."

"Know it all? I was Miss Know Nothing. I was a wild child. I got knocked-up in high school. My mom and dad had saved up enough money and rather than keep me in Cleveland they up and moved to Detroit. Dad bought a liquor store/market, a nice house, and mamma stayed home with my daughter while I went out and worked."

"As a maid in Grosse Point," I said.

"That's right, as a maid in Grosse Point. And I was a damn good maid, 'cause my mamma wouldn't let me do otherwise."

"I'll bet you were," Dango said smiling.

"How'd you end up here?" I asked.

"Met Big Lou at the family where I worked. He was the chauffeur and cook, if you can believe that. He was also a deacon at the church where we all went and he loved Charlie."

"Charlie?" I said.

"Charlene, my daughter. My daddy said if I didn't marry Lou he'd kick me out of the house anyways. So that's what I did. Lou has family down here, knew this place was for sale so we bought it."

"You're the owners here?" Chuck asked.

"Damn right and doing real well, thank you very much."

"Do a lot better if you didn't talk so much," said Big Lou in a deep voice. He had drifted over unnoticed. "We need to clean up, so we can close up."

Reola punched him gently in the stomach as she stood. "You take care, old man. I'll cut you off," she said as she started clearing the plates.

"Food okay, guys?" Big Lou asked.

"More than okay," Dango said. "You see anything left?"

Dango was right. No one had left a thing on their plates.

Lou smiled. "We aims to please. Come back next time through. Tell your friends."

"We will," said Chuck.

Reola came back to the table with the bill. We each chipped in a five, which more than covered it with enough left over for a good tip. I gave Reola the money as she stood there with Lou and the others started to the door.

"Where's Charlie now?" I asked before I headed out.

"Michigan State," she said with a smile. "Junior in Sociology."

Big Lou came up and put his arm around her shoulder. Dango and I turned back and waved after we went out the door. Chuck was waiting for us by the Bel Air. He already had the back driver's side door open.

"You going to take the first shift, Lee?" he said holding out the keys.

I looked at Dango, saw he wasn't offering, so I took the keys.

"Guess so," I said. "Since I got a couple hours of sleep."

"I'll sit up front with you and catch a few zzzs," Dango said. "And I'll be ready to go when you get tired."

"Great," Chuck said as he flopped in the backseat. "I'm gonna get at least a couple of hours. No need of any directions - straight shot to St. Louis, just stay on 66."

I started the car, looked both ways and headed back out on to 66.

Dango looked over at me from the passenger seat.

"You okay?" he said.

"For a while," I answered. "You better get some sleep, so you can take the next leg."

"Don't worry. I'm gone," he said as he leaned back and shut his eyes.

There was very little traffic on 66 at this hour. Hardly any cars, but a good number of big semis. Chuck kept his Bel Air in good shape and it purred right along at 70. Most of the time 66 was four lanes, but for some stretches and through towns, it would drop to two and I'd have to slow down if I was behind one of the big trucks. Every once in a while, I'd get passed by a Corvette or a Lincoln Town Car. There were even a couple of semis that barreled past me on long straightaways. When I saw one of those babies coming up behind me in the rearview mirror, and when it flashed its bright lights, I'd slow down quick and let it pass. I had fantasies of those giant chrome grills on the Macks opening up and swallowing the Bel Air whole instead of passing.

I found it funny that I should be driving again on this trip, when the reason we were even here was because I'd driven my car off the road. I kept the radio playing low and was able to pick up Wolfman Jack playing his Rock 'n' Roll selections. I have no idea where the Wolfman broadcast from, or how his signal seemed to reach from California all the way to Chicago, but it did. The rumor was he broadcast from Mexico near the border to beat FCC regulations about signal power. I imagined a radio tower somewhere as tall as the Empire State Building.

The alone-time driving gave me a chance to think back on the day just passed. The distance traveled was remarkable, but what made it memorable was the people we'd met. I wondered why Reola had just decided to tell so much about herself to two white teenage hitchhikers who came in off the road late one night. Why, for that matter, had Ron and Chuck and almost everyone who picked us up, felt like they could tell us anything about themselves after knowing us for just a few minutes? I remember coming to the conclusion that it had everything to do with the certainty they'd never see us again.

I could tell as I drove, even at night, that the landscape was changing. There were fewer long stretches of straight highway. The road began to climb and curve more. The Bel Air's headlights would flash by signs that said "Ozark this" and "Ozark that." Bright boy that I was, I figured we'd entered the Ozarks. I also realized I'd probably never see them at this hour. The change of terrain meant I definitely had to concentrate more on the driving. I cracked the window open a bit to let in the air. The temperature had dropped and, with the cool air hitting the warm land, I'd run into pockets of fog on the highway. I'd have to slow down and dim the lights as the visibility dropped. I had just passed through the town of Lebanon, which I figured was about halfway through the state, when I first felt my eyes get heavy. I'd been driving for about an hour and a half on a very full stomach. I sat straight up and tightened my grip on the wheel. I kicked the sleeping Dango on the foot.

"Hey," I said. "Start getting up. Next town, you're taking over."

"What time is it?" he said, rubbing his eyes.

"After two, I think."

"Where are we?"

"Halfway to St. Louis. Last sign I saw said 150 some miles."

"Okay, pull off when you can, I'm ready," Dango said. "But find a place where I can take a leak."

The next town came up in 10 miles: "Waynesville, Missouri. Gateway to Fort Leonard Wood." Of course, nothing was open. I pulled into the deserted gravel parking lot of a Stuckey's, a chain of restaurants that seemed to be everywhere in Missouri, pushing peanut brittle. I stopped the Bel Air by some brush at the side of the parking lot and shut it off. I opened my door. The silence was deafening. Dango and I looked into the backseat. Chuck had scrunched himself, legs folded, so he fit perfectly, head into the seat, sleeping soundly. Dango and I exited the Chevy quietly, went over to the brush and unzipped our flies.

"Boy, it's cooled off," he said, watching the steam rise from his piss.

"Yeah, you gotta watch it," I answered. "There's been a little fog on the road."

"I'm ready," he said, zipping up. "Let's go."

After leaving Waynesville, Route 66 went completely dark as it passed Fort Leonard Wood to the south. The fort seemed to go on for miles.

"God, this thing is huge," I said.

"We've already gone eight miles and I don't see an end to it," Dango said.

"I don't see anything," I said, looking into the blackness.

I had no idea then, that in six years, I'd see more of Fort Leonard Wood than I'd ever want to. But, six years was a lifetime away. Now all I wanted to do was get some sleep. I looked in back; Chuck was on his back snoring peacefully. I looked over at Dango.

"You good?"

"I got Wolfman on the radio. We're gonna be in Cleveland tomorrow and then the party starts. I'm great. Get some sleep."

I smiled, put my head down on the seat by the passenger door, kept my feet on the floor and shut my eyes. It was the last time in my life that I have ever been able to sleep in a car.

The same sound. The same sound woke me up again. Tires running too fast over gravel. I started to raise my head then, suddenly, the Chevy swerved to the left, first throwing me into the passenger door then onto the floor on the passenger side. The car bumped along at what seemed like an incredible speed. I could see Dango's feet and legs as he tried to brake. The car hit something hard on the left side and there was an awful scraping sound. I was experiencing Sequoia all over again, except now I was in Billy Pancetti's spot. It was in slow motion again, and what must have been seconds seemed minutes. After the hit on the passenger side, the car turned that way and felt like it was going to roll. Dango must have turned the wheel or something because I could feel the tires on my side hit the ground. But now we seemed headed downhill. Definitely not on pavement. Dango must have been able to find the brake and kill the engine because the Chevy slowed and then stopped – facing downhill, tilted to the driver's side.

"Lee, you alright?" I heard Dango shout.

"I think so," I said, crawling back up into the seat. "You?"

"I fell asleep, damn it!" he said.

"I figured," I said angrily as I pulled myself up further and looked into the backseat.

There was no one there. The back driver's side door was wide open. The freshly pressed uniform was still hanging on the hook above the door into the empty space. There was no Chuck.

"Dango, Chuck's gone," I shouted.

He looked in back then opened his door and jumped out. Since the car was tilting that way, I sort of rolled out after him.

I fell into some very deep grass and as I scrambled to my feet, I looked around to get my bearings. It wasn't dark, but it wasn't light. That strange gray semi-light before dawn made even grayer by a dense fog. All I could tell was we had obviously gone off the side of Route 66 and come to a stop on a grassy slope. Above me, I heard the deep engine noise of a semi. I looked up and saw the lights and dark shape of a giant truck rumble by.

Dango was crawling up the slope trying to follow the track of the car. I followed him, yelling, "Chuck! Chuck!"

We came to a power pole disappearing up into the fog. You could see the red paint where the Chevy had hit it on the way down. This is where the door must have opened and Chuck fell out, but there was still no sign of him.

Dango kept yelling and I joined in: "Chuck! Chuck!"

When we reached the edge of the highway, suddenly, through the fog, a big set of headlights started flashing at us and the loudest horn I ever heard sounded three times. Another semi, headed the same direction as the last, loomed in front of us then roared past, way too close for comfort. I had a gruesome thought for a second of what a truck like that would do to a body thrown into its path.

Then, through the fog, Dango and I saw the silhouette of a man, stumbling toward us along the same side of the highway we were on.

"Chuck!" Dango shouted again and ran toward him.

Dango reached him, grabbed him, hugged him by the shoulders and started to guide him back away from the highway. The lights and noise of another semi passed above us as they got to where I was standing.

All Dango kept saying was, "Chuck, Chuck, Chuck."

I looked at him closely, face to face, "Are you alright?"

As far as I could tell he was alright. In fact, I didn't see a scratch on him. He must have landed in the deep grass when the car went off the highway and before it hit the pole.

"What happened?" he asked, his voice a little wobbly.

"I fell asleep," Dango said. "The car went off the road."

Chuck looked at him for a second as Dango's words registered.

"My Chevy! My Chevy! Is the Chevy okay?" he shouted.

"It's fine, it's fine," Dango answered. "C'mon."

Dango, holding Chuck around the shoulders, guided him down the hill, toward the power pole, toward the '57 Bel Air. I just stood there stunned and shook my head. Chuck was obviously "fine." After what must have been one of the most frightening experiences I could imagine – being thrown from your car and awakening in a dense fog on the ground next to the major cross-country highway in the United States, and then almost getting run over by a giant semi – he had regained his senses and had his priorities straight: he was worried about his '57 Chevy Bel Air.

I followed them back down the slope, pretty sure of two things: One, the Chevy wasn't "fine." Two, we were all lucky to be alive. A little hazy sunlight was beginning to filter through the fog as I reached them. Chuck was on his haunches staring at the driver's side of the car. Dango was standing next to him. The Bel Air had sideswiped the power pole, starting at the front fender running all the way to the back fender. I was no expert on bodywork, but I knew the work needed on Chuck's Bel Air was going to be more than the car was worth. Hell, my Star Chief, after dropping 15 feet off the road, looked better than Chuck's Bel Air.

"It's just body damage," Dango said. "It drives fine."

There was that word "fine" again. Nothing was "fine."

Chuck just stared at the side of the car. I thought for a second that he might be crying.

"Look, I'll help pay for it," Dango said, trying to make him feel better.

"Okay, maybe you can," Chuck said as he stood up. "Let's get into St. Louis. How far is it?"

"About 25 miles, I think," Dango said.

"I'll drive," Chuck said, which has to go down as one of the all-time remarks that didn't need to be made.

I was amazed at Chuck's lack of emotion during this whole situation. I think even I would have tried to beat Dango to a pulp, if he'd done this to me. Maybe Chuck was in shock. Or, maybe his years as a clerk in the Army had taken all the fight out of him. Dango and I helped push the car, so the tires could get some traction going up the grassy slope. As the fog lifted, you could begin to see how lucky we had been. Route 66 had split into a divided highway as it passed through the last of the Ozarks on its way into St. Louis. Dango must have fallen asleep and started to drift off the highway to the right. Awakened by the gravel, he jerked the steering wheel to the left and the Bel Air then jumped back across the two lanes, went off the other side and sideswiped the power pole, which probably kept it from rolling over as it headed down the grassy median.

We picked up the driver's side outdoor rearview mirror, which we found by the power pole and put it on the floor of the backseat. The only other repair we had to make was to the rear door on the driver's side. It wouldn't close all the way or lock. We took the wire hanger from Chuck's uniform to jerry-rig it shut. Just as the sun started to break up the last of the fog, Chuck floored his Bel Air and we hopped back on Route 66 from the median side of the highway.

No one said much on those last few miles into St. Louis.

CHAPTER 8

Cleveland – Summer of 1962

We named it the "sleeping hole" – that was the one-room-and-bath that Dango and I shared in the summer of 1962. It was in the Coventry/Mayfield section of Cleveland Heights, just on the border where Mayfield Road dropped down into the city. Kind of the slum of Cleveland Heights, if Cleveland Heights had a slum. The "apartment" was located on a side street just off Coventry in the basement of a 12-unit apartment building of four floors. I don't think they counted our sleeping hole as one of the units. The rent was $75 a month and that seemed steep considering the lack of amenities. There were two single beds, a desk with a lamp and a hot plate, a small closet and a window that opened to a sunken window well. You had to walk over right to the window and look up if you wanted to see the sky. The bathroom had a sink, mirror, one light bulb and a tiny stall shower with plastic curtain. The tent/shack we shared in Sequoia was more spacious and much nicer. But, for the summer of 1962, the sleeping hole suited Dango and me just fine.

After my freshman year at Claremont Men's College, I had pleaded with my parents, now living in San Francisco, to let me return to Cleveland for one more summer. Even though I had made new friends at Claremont, I knew no one in "the city by the bay," and the idea of spending a summer there, tied to my parents, seemed the ultimate in boredom. Dango and I had communicated, mostly by postcards from Rutgers to Claremont, during the school year and hatched the plan to room together. I contacted the machine shop where I worked in the summer of '60 and got my old job back. I guess finding workers for minimum wage, willing to drill endless holes in burners for hot water heaters, wasn't easy. Once I had the job, my parents reluctantly agreed to my returning to Cleveland for the summer, and as soon as I was on board, Dango's mother agreed to let him room with me. She liked me, and trusted me. She believed I would be a good influence on her son: "Why can't you be more like Lee, Bob?" was her mantra.

A week and a half after Memorial Day in June, I left San Francisco in the 1955 Karmann Ghia my parents had given me so that I would have wheels at Claremont. It had over 100,000 miles on it, but it was the original VW bug engine in a low-slung "sports car" body; it would run forever. I took one of my new college friends to his home in Denver, and then continued on to Cleveland. Crossing the country in the Ghia was slower than hitchhiking. The little 4–cylinder engine barely got the speed up to 55 mph on any kind of grade. Straightaways, pedal to the floor, you might hit 70. If I felt threatened by big rigs in the '57 Chevy of Chuck's, imagine my fear as the giant trucks came barreling up behind the low-riding, under-powered Ghia. Humility became a driving strategy.

I pulled into Cleveland after five days on the road and stayed at Dango's home one night. We found the sleeping hole in one day and moved in two hours after pre-paying the first month's rent. Needless to say, none of our parents ever saw the basement den; they just knew we had rented a one bedroom apartment. Their boys were growing up.

Actually, "their boys" were doing the opposite. The sleeping hole allowed Dango and me one last summer of clinging with a vengeance to the irresponsible freedom of childhood.

During the days we worked. Dango ran his tree trimming crew and I drove out by the interstate to punch the time clock at my machine shop. When we got off work, we met at a local bar on the corner of Coventry and Mayfield, shared a few beers and made plans for the evenings. Sometimes, if one of us had a date for the night, we'd split up, but most of the time we drove to a friend's house for parties or get-togethers. We never once turned on the hot plate in our room. We either ate at the corner bar, at some fast food joint or mooched dinner at a friend's house. Many evenings ended at the bar, closing it at 2:00 a.m. and walking the three blocks back to the sleeping hole. Waking at 7:00 a.m. to get to my job, I learned to live with the morning hangovers. I would stop at a small coffee shop every morning on the way to work for a quick breakfast of black coffee and a doughnut or bacon and egg sandwich. Egg McMuffins were years away. In the first month, I fell asleep four times on the drill press at my job, snapping four extra heavy-duty steel drill bits. They moved me to sorting parts and packing boxes. I marvel now when I imagine how Dango must have felt swinging from branch to branch, high in the elms, heavy chainsaw in hand, after nights of closing our local bar. Hangover took on a whole new meaning.

As the summer progressed, each weekend seemed to get wilder and drunker than the last. It was as if the University School graduating class of 1961 knew they were on borrowed time. They had extended the party to another summer and, without any of us expressing it to any of the others, there was a shared feeling that it couldn't – and shouldn't – last much longer.

It was during one of those weekends, in the middle of August, that Dango more than repaid his backseat Eldorado sexual encounter debt to me. And saved my life in the process.

After sleeping late Saturday in our sleeping hole, we went out to a late breakfast/brunch with Dango's Rutgers roommate, Big John AuWerter. John let us know that there was going to be a party that evening at another '61 grad's house, Kyle Miller. There was going to be a party at Kyle's house for the same reason there was a party at anyone's house – the parents were out of town. Fortified with that knowledge, and not having to spend any more time figuring out what we were going to do for the evening, we went pool-hopping around Shaker Heights and at 7:00 p.m., headed back to our room to shower and put on relatively clean clothes for the party.

The Miller's was a relatively new, ranch-style, wood frame house with a large yard just off Fairmont Boulevard, east of Lee Road. Wood frame houses were unusual in the Heights, and most that existed were architecturally interesting just to compete with the other mansions. The Miller's home was a large, rambling two-story house with a big rec room built over the three-car garage. When Dango and I got there about 8:30, it was still light and the party was mainly concentrated in the backyard, kitchen, and rec room. All the kids just knew instinctively not to mess up the nicer living areas. After all, when you threw the next party at your parentless house, you'd expect the same consideration. All in all, there must have been about 75 college-age revelers at the height of the party around 11:30 p.m. Kyle's younger sister, Kate, who was nicknamed Cat and was still in high school, had about eight of her friends over too. There were two kegs going. Everyone was drinking. A lot.

It dawns on me now that what might be considered irresponsible at 18 might be inexcusable at 19. But I had no sense of that back then. Even though Dango and I logged many miles together across country and had one year of college under our belt, in 1962, growing up was a long way off. If, indeed, it was ever achieved.

I know this much now and I knew it then: Kyle's sister Cat was beautiful, fully developed and only 16. By about 12:45 in the morning, the crowd had diminished and there were only about 15 hard partiers left. Everyone gathered in the rec room, except for a few heavy daters that were somewhere in the backyard. Dango had paired off with a girlfriend of Kyle's girlfriend and I was the odd man out. Cat had had quite a bit to drink and all her high school friends had left. The group in the rec room was listening to a Miles Davis album sipping their last beers and smoking. Kyle had acquired a taste for jazz his first year at Wooster. I was sitting on an ottoman near Dango and his new friend, Cat was sitting on a couch across from us next to her brother and his girl. She had on short shorts which displayed an incredible set of tanned legs and all she did was stare at me through two of those long Miles Davis cuts. I could see she was drunk. I was feeling no pain myself, but I figured it was time to get out. I asked Dango if he could get a ride back to our basement off Coventry. He said "No problem," and so I left the rec room and headed toward the front of the house.

Halfway down the stairs to the first floor, Cat caught up with me.

"Lee, wait a sec. I'll walk you out."

She grabbed my hand and, instead of leading me to the front door, led me out to the backyard. She stopped once at the patio, turned to me, put her arms around my neck and kissed me. The kiss, the body pressing tight against me, and the way it all moved together suggested more experience in lovemaking than a mere 16 years. But I knew. I knew she was 16; I knew she was the sister of a friend; I knew it was a bad idea; and I knew it was wrong. It didn't stop me for a second. After that kiss, I took her by the hand, led her into that large backyard and we looked for a place to lie down behind some large azalea bushes. The big white flowers shone like neon in the dark night. We hit the grass. Her short shorts and panties were off in a second. I think she took care of that, while I got my jeans and boxers down to my ankles. In a few more seconds, we were doing what young oversexed animals do best. And I will tell you something: young Cat Miller was no virgin and probably had more on-the-job training than her older legally adult partner. I keep remembering that night in seconds. It all seemed that fast. It must have at least been minutes, though, because right in the middle of our teenage backyard passion, I heard Kyle yelling from the patio.

"Katey, Katey . . . are you out here?"

I froze, pushed up on my hands and, through the azalea branches, could see Kyle and his girlfriend begin to walk down into the yard.

I rolled off Cat and reached down to pull up my pants.

"Cat, quick, put on your clothes," I whispered. "I'll go try to stall them."

"Huh," she grunted, a little dazed.

Pants on and zippered, I got up and started walking toward the couple. I just hoped they'd think I'd been out in the back taking a leak. When you panic, you'll hope anything.

Kyle saw me.

"Lee, you seen Kate?"

"Yeah, I think she's in the kitchen," I lied.

"Oh, okay," he said, and they turned back toward the house.

I walked with them back to the patio.

"Thanks for tonight, Kyle. I'm headed back to our basement," I said. "Maybe you can give Dango a ride?"

"Sure thing."

I gave a short wave and headed for the front door. I was running. I got to the Ghia and was headed down Fairmont in no time. In a half hour, I was in my sleeping hole, breathing a sigh of relief, thinking I'd just gotten away with another close one. An hour later, I'd know how very wrong I was.

I woke up to Dango pounding on our apartment door. He had a key, why didn't he just let himself in?

"Lee, Lee, open up, I need your help," Dango shouted.

I hopped out of bed and opened the door. Facing me were Dango and Kyle Miller. Kyle was holding his right arm up close to his chest. Wrapped around his right hand was what looked like a white blood-covered T-shirt?

"What's happening?" I asked.

"I'll tell you after you help me take Kyle to Mayfield Hospital Emergency," he said looking at me hard. "But first, tell him you didn't rape his sister."

"Rape his sister?" I choked out.

"Tell him," he said angrily.

"I didn't rape anyone," I said, I hoped convincingly.

"See, I told you, Kyle," Dango said. "Now come on, Lee, drive Kyle's car up to Mayfield Hospital. I'll sit in back with him."

Kyle spoke for the first time. He sounded a little woozy. "I'm sorry, Lee. I just went a little crazy. Too much to drink, I think."

"What happened?" I asked again.

"I'll tell you in the car. Get your clothes on," Dango snapped.

But Dango didn't tell me in the car. He sat in the back of the Miller's Ford station wagon, talking quietly to Kyle. I drove the short 12 or so blocks up Mayfield to the hospital in about five minutes. The only clue I had as to what had led up to this emergency room visit, was a large, single-blade, German kitchen knife with blood on it lying in the middle of the front passenger seat.

I dropped Dango and Kyle at the emergency room door and went to park the car. I came back to the empty waiting room and after a few minutes Dango came out and sat with me.

"Jesus, man," he said. "What did you do?"

I related to him my backyard escapade with Cat Miller, making sure to point out I had done nothing he wouldn't have done.

Dango just shook his head and told me what had happened: "After you left, all hell broke loose. They found Cat in the backyard, stumbling around - and this I had to see to believe - she had her shorts on, but her panties were around her ankles. I don't know how you do that. She was drunk and incoherent, so the girls put her to bed. Then Kyle grabbed me and said, 'We're gonna take the girls home and go find Livingston.' I just kept my mouth shut and went along for the ride. After we dropped the girls off, we started heading for the apartment and I can see he's a little mad and crazy. He looked like he was going to break the steering wheel. So I asked him what was wrong. The girls had told him you raped his sister. I asked if he'd talked to Cat. He said 'No', but he was going to kill you anyway. I never knew Kyle ever cared about any girl's honor, but there we were heading down to get you and I'm trying to talk some sense into his head, to get him to slow down and think. And then I see this goddamn butcher's knife next to him on the seat. I say,

'What's that for?' He says, 'Livingston.' So I grab it by the handle to get it away from him and he reaches over with his right hand to get it from me and grabs the blade. Sploooey, blood all over the place. Thank God I had a T-shirt on. We pull over, I wrap his hand and then he begins to sober up and settle down. You know the rest."

"Does he still think I raped her?" I asked.

"I don't know," Dango said. "I think he's okay. Probably more worried about his hand. But look, the story we told the docs in there was he cut his hand on a beer bottle that exploded. So if anyone asks you, that's the story. We don't want them thinking we were in some kind of gang fight."

Seemed like a pretty smart story for about five minutes, until two of Cleveland Heights' finest walked into the emergency room. The police walked over to the nurse at the desk, talked to her for a minute and then she pointed over to us.

The ride from Mayfield Hospital to the Cleveland Heights Police Station was only about three blocks. At least they didn't put us in cuffs. As soon as Kyle was released from the emergency room with his stitched and bandaged hand, they put the three of us in the back of the squad car for the short trip to the station. It was a quick booking. I never did find out the exact charge they originally booked us on, but by 3:00 a.m. we were each in separate jail cells. I tried to get some sleep, but my mind was bouncing all over the place trying to figure out what happened and more worrisome, what was going to happen. The big mistake had been making up a story about a beer bottle breaking and causing a cut. The doctors knew a knife wound when they saw one and had immediately called the police. The police had gotten some kind of statement from Kyle, then decided to book us all for the night for questioning. Something happened, someone had a pretty serious knife injury – they were going to get to the bottom of it. Meanwhile, from 3:00 a.m. to daybreak, the three of us were the only occupants of the Cleveland Heights jail. The only sound was the ticking of a large clock above the doorway at the end of the hallway between the cells. The only light came from a couple of phosphorescent ceiling lights in the hall. Each cell had a toilet without a fold-up seat, a washbasin and a fold-down cot. It was eerie, depressing and cold – just the way a jail should be. 10 minutes after they put us in, Dango and Kyle were sound asleep – the sleep of the innocent. I never slept.

At what I guessed to be about 8:00 a.m., you could hear increased activity outside the cellblock. Half an hour after that, a uniformed officer and what I suspected was a plainclothes cop entered. They called Kyle's name and Bob's name from a clipboard. They opened their cells and took them out. Dango looked at me as they headed toward the door. I wondered if I looked as scared as he looked, and I knew he had that look for me.

At 9:00 a.m., they brought me a small metal tray with a breakfast of powdered eggs, toast and orange juice. I drank the juice. It wasn't until about 11 in the morning that two plainclothes detectives came to get me. The detectives took me to an interrogation room with just a table, chair and a large wall mirror. It looked like the room in every cop TV show where they interview people.

The detectives looked like every cop in those shows, too. They both had their jackets off, wore white shirts with the cuffs rolled up, and had one button on the collar undone with a loose tie. The shorter, dark-haired detective did all the talking. His name was Gianelli.

"You know why you're here?" he asked.

"No, Sir," I responded, hoping I didn't.

"You're held under suspicion of statutory rape."

So much for hope. I just looked at him. I had nothing to say.

"That's a pretty serious charge, Lee," he said. "Can I call you Lee?"

I nodded.

"Why don't you start at the beginning and tell me what happened last night. Your side of it, anyway." He looked me straight in the eyes. He'd taken out a small green spiral notebook, which he put on the table in front of him. I figured him to be about forty, forty-five. I saw a wedding band. I had a hunch he was a father. So that's how I talked to him: like he was my father and I'd just made a big mistake. I told him the whole story the way I remembered it. I didn't try to make myself look good and I didn't paint Cat as an innocent little girl. He listened, took notes occasionally. His partner lit a cigarette.

When I finished, I put my hands together on the table and looked right at him. He leaned back and stared straight back at me.

"Did you consummate the intercourse?"

"What do you mean?"

"Did you ejaculate? Did you come?"

"I'm not sure," I replied. "I don't know. It all happened so fast."

He leaned forward, putting his hands back on the table. He talked softly, I thought, almost kindly.

"I tell ya, Lee, you're in a tough spot. Jerry and I here are both fathers, but we're both men, too. I've seen some of these 16-year-old girls. You got caught up in the moment; you got more hormones running around than you know what to do with. So does she. That's why my kids go to Catholic school. They got priests and nuns walking around with yardsticks to whack most of those hormones silly and load the others up with guilt."

"I'm just telling you this so you understand: we sympathize with you. I'm not even sure it's a good law, but it's a law and this is the way it's gonna go down: The Millers are taking Katherine to their doctor at one today to be examined. If they find anything, and you know what I mean by find anything, right?"

I nodded again.

"Then you'll be charged. If they don't find anything, we let you go. That simple."

He looked at me and smiled.

"So there's nothing you can do, nothing we can do, but wait. But Livingston – I know you're not Catholic, but you might try praying."

With that, the interview or interrogation or whatever you want to call it was over. They took me back to my cell. I didn't have to call my parents in California; I didn't have to get a lawyer, yet. I just had to wait. So that's what I did. And I did pray.

At 3:00 p.m., Gianelli came and got me.

"You can go," was all he said. "Your buddy's here to pick you up. God smiled on you."

I went outside of the cellblock. Dango was standing by the front desk. I almost ran to him and kissed him, but I kept my cool 'til we got outside. I actually started crying. Dango put his arm around me, led me to the Ghia and drove us home to our basement room.

A best friend in high school is not a best friend for the conversations you have; he's a best friend for the conversations you don't have. I didn't have to hear from Dango how stupid I'd been, or how lucky I'd been, or how wild I was; I only needed to have him there. He'd picked me up out of that jail the same way I'd picked him out of the snow bank. We never, as I recall, really discussed what I had been thinking. I remember times when we laughed about it later. Another story, another close call. But I knew he understood everything I went through and if positions had been reversed, I knew, he would have been on Cat Miller in a second.

You would have thought an experience like that would have dampened Dango's and my party spirit for the rest of the summer. It did, for about a week. But as August 1962 drew to a close and everyone started to get ready to head back to college for their sophomore year, Dango and I came up with the perfect idea for the party to end all parties. At least, the party to end the summer.

My parents still owned the second lot next to our old house on Berkshire Drive. It was actually an extension of the backyard and ran all the way to the next street over, Derbyshire Drive. It was on the corner of Derbyshire and a small neighborhood alley. The full lot had magnificent mature elms and maples, and on the corner with the alley, a fenced-in clay tennis court. (Yes, I had a tennis court growing up. We fixed it up one year and I took lessons, but I hated the sport, and for most of the years we lived there the court was used to store compost.) A small fence ran from the tennis court to the next property on Derbyshire. At the junction of the small fence and the tennis court was a small locked gate, which I had the key to. Why my father had given me the key, I have no idea. I'm sure, though, it was not to throw the party to end all parties.

Dango, always the entrepreneur, came up with the idea to make the party a profitable business venture. $3 per head at the gate to get in, $5 for couples. We planned it for the Friday night of Labor Day weekend. After Labor Day, the exodus back to colleges would begin. We got the word out to all our University School friends and even printed some single-sheet flyers for them to pass out to other friends.

Dango and I skipped work on that Friday and prepared for the event. He used his truck from the tree service to pick up the 10 kegs of beer from the local brewery – Carling's. They made Carling's Black Label, a beer almost undrinkable from the bottle, but tolerable ice-cold from the keg. Not one of our college guzzlers would mind or care. We also used the truck to pick up four tubs to ice the kegs, block ice from the Union Ice House, and a sizable gas-powered generator for lights and a stereo system. From one in the afternoon Friday until 6:00 p.m., Dango, myself and three other University School buddies from his tree crew, prepared the party site.

Most of my preparation work consisted of going, very sweetly, to the immediate neighbors and "preparing" them for the party. I knew them from having lived there for years, and I assured them we would stick strictly to the lot, that it would be over by 1:00 a.m. and that we would be sure to clean up. There was such a large distance between the lot and the houses nearby we hoped noise would not be a problem. Dango and the other guys set up the party, hanging lights in the trees and on the fences, putting up a large folding table in front of two kegs on ice in the tennis court to act as a bar. Behind the kegs was another table where one of Dango's crew ran a tape recorder and small stereo sound-system. Wires went to two large speakers hung high up on the tennis court fence facing the main party area. The generator was far back in the tennis court, near the compost heap, so no one would hear it or see it.

I don't think I can ever recall Dango being happier than when he was giving orders and working his tail off to get the "Last Party" ready. I provided the property, but this was his party. He was the organizer and, in his mind, he was doing it so all our friends could have a great ending to the summer.

At eight o'clock, the late summer sun low in the sky, we turned on the tape recorder and the first guests began to arrive at the gate. Dango and I, as the hosts, alternated between taking money at the gate and walking the party to make sure everything was going okay. We had a couple of the bigger guys from the defensive line of University School's 1961 undefeated football team standing by if there was any sign of trouble.

No trouble ever erupted. At least, not the kind we expected. Kids came from University School, Laurel and Hathaway Brown, of course. But somehow word had reached Cleveland Heights and Shaker Heights High School and even further out to high schools in Parma and Pepper Pike. Dango came to me at one point in the festivities and said a couple of guys and their dates had shown up from the west side of Cleveland – unheard of for a party in the east side Heights. Amazingly, everyone seemed to be just laying back, drinking their beer and enjoying themselves. Dango had made a deal with Dante's, the local pizza emporium down on Coventry, so they were shuffling multi orders of pizza to the backyard all during the party. How much money they made, I'll never know. I always had a hunch Dango made himself a little extra on the side from Dante's, too. Dango was a born entrepreneur, always making deals. He should have run a company; maybe a big construction company where he could be outdoors, running around giving orders and building things. He was happy building things.

The only trouble we had at the party was the size. We stopped taking money at ten o'clock and we had over $600. We figured the crowd at around 350. The large backyard was filled and there were even kids standing in the compost heap behind the makeshift bar. Dango and I hadn't stopped for a second. As co-hosts we kept making sure the beer was flowing, trash bags were picked-up, and the music tapes uninterrupted. At 10:30, we were well into the 7th and 8th keg when one of Dango's crew let us know where the problem was going to be.

"Hey you guys," he said as he came running up. "The street's jammed with cars. There's no place to park."

Dango and I went over to the back gate and looked out onto Derbyshire Drive. Sure enough, there were cars packed with kids going both ways on the street. It looked like a crowd down at Municipal Stadium lining up to get into a Cleveland Browns game.

We sent crew members from car to car, telling drivers to head over to Cedar Blvd, a major street one block over, to try and park in one of the church parking lots. In the early '60s, most church, school and building parking lots were open and accessible after hours. As the traffic jam began to break up, Dango and I walked back through the partiers to the bar and had our second glass of beer. Looking out over the large crowd of happy revelers, softly lit from the lights sparkling in the trees above, he toasted me.

"Here's to the best damn party of any summer."

We touched our large paper beer cups and I, always the realist, toasted back.

"I don't know if it's the 'best,' but it's damn well the biggest."

Dango didn't miss a beat when he came back with the capper, "And we've got about 15 minutes before the cops come to close it down."

He was off about half an hour. At 11:30 the defensive lineman who'd been watching the gate came to get me.

"Lee," he said. "There are a couple of cops here asking for the owner of the property."

"I'll be right there," I said.

I quickly found Dango and told him that what we had both expected had arrived. He began to go through the crowd and pass the word. I went to the gate. There was a plainclothes and uniformed cop waiting for me.

"You the owner?" the plainclothes cop asked.

"Yes sir," I said. "It's my family's property."

"Oh no . . ." I heard him say, as he shone a flashlight on my face. "Livingston!"

I jumped when I heard the voice, my first instinct was to turn, run back into the party and hide. But then I sucked it up and tried to play it cool: "Good evening, Lieutenant Gianelli."

"I thought I saw the last of you two weeks ago," he said. "I thought you'd be in California."

"Not going 'til next week," I answered, trying to keep it friendly.

"Not soon enough for me. How many kids you got in there?" he asked nodding to the packed backyard.

"A couple of hundred, I think."

He looked at me and shook his head.

"It's amazing. We've had no complaints about the party. Just the cars and traffic and parking. I suppose if I went in there I could arrest some of the sons and daughters of the best families in Cleveland and Shaker Heights for underage drinking. But you guys have probably figured out I'm not going to do that. So here's what we will do . . ."

He paused for a moment, looked at his watch and then back at me.

"It's 11:35 now. You've got half an hour to clear this place out quietly, neatly. Cops will be patrolling. Any drinking or littering on public streets and we'll take people in. I'll come back after 12 to check. You got it?"

"Yes, sir."

"Oh, cut the polite crap, Livingston. Just do it." He turned and walked into the dark.

It didn't take a lot of urging on Dango's and my part to get people to start leaving. Word had spread quickly that the cops had shown up, everyone polished off their last draft and started to file out. We made sure to collect cups and warn the exiting partiers to keep it down. The crowd of kids was remarkably good-natured about the party breaking up. I think they figured that four hours for a major beer blast in the center of Cleveland Heights before the cops broke it up was a major success.

By midnight, only Dango and I and a few of our best University School friends were left to finish the clean-up. We were draining the seventh and eighth keg and all sharing the last few beers to salute our triumph when Lieutenant Gianelli walked into the backyard. Dango took one of the last paper cups filled with beer and offered it to him.

"Want a beer, Lieutenant?" Dango said with a smile.

Gianelli stopped in his tracks and just stared at Dango.

"You are a piece of work, Mr. Lyons. Toss that away before I put you in jail . . . again."

Gianelli took a moment to survey the remnants of the party. Then he looked beyond the lights to the big Berkshire house in the background.

"This where you used to live, Livingston?"

"This is the place," I said.

"How many rooms in that house?" he asked.

"A lot. Over 30, I think."

He looked back at me. He had that same look on his face that he'd had back in the interrogation room when he'd told me to pray. "You've been very lucky this summer, Livingston. Looks like you've been lucky all your life. Don't keep pushing it."

He turned and started to walk out.

"All of you guys," he said without turning back. "Get out of here."

We closed it down and left. But about 25 of us, the hard-core friends and drinkers from the University School class of '61 started a new party the next day. We had to – we had two kegs of beer left to kill.

Off a side road, deep in the woods, in the country near Chagrin Falls, Ohio, we had discovered a large outcropping of rock we dubbed "Whippling Rock." We had taken kegs out there our senior year for beer busts and no one ever bothered us, so it seemed a fitting place to end the summer and say good-bye. Most all the kids who gathered were heading back to their colleges the next week. Dango and I drove out with the two leftover kegs in his tree service truck.

From the road where we all parked, you hiked about a quarter mile to the base of the rock. Its jagged front went straight up about 55 feet into the tall trees. There were boulders strewn at the base that we could sit and lean against to enjoy our beers. One of the lower boulders made the perfect perch for the ice tubs and keg. We called it Whippling Rock because when our bladders became full, we'd walk around the side and find crevices to pee in. One year, two of the guys had found a way to climb up the back of the sloping rock to the top, unzip and pee down on the guzzlers at the base. High school humor.

It only took an hour for the twenty or so of us to polish off the first keg. At the huge party the night before, everyone had been on their best behavior, but now, deep in the woods, summer almost over, we all let go. Mid-afternoon, the heat and humidity, even in the shaded woods, was unbearable. You started sweating the minute you started drinking.

Every other cold beer was used to give one of your buddies a beer shower. All of us were having beer fights and throwing loose pieces of ice from the tub at each other by the time the second keg was tapped. Half of us had our shirts off and the other half had beer-soaked shirts.

We were all having a great time and partying hard. We started to make plans to go to the nearby Chagrin River to cool off and clean up as soon as the second keg was done.

No one had noticed but Dango had drifted off with the '61 senior class President of University School, George Grabner. Now, these were two great guys, both fun to hang out with, but both, when they drank too much, didn't know when to stop. They had walked around to the back of Whippling Rock and then up to the top. You would expect the two of them to shower their classmates below, or maybe dare each other to jump and have us try to catch them as they cheated death; but no, as fate would have it, they found something else stupid to do. The top of the giant rock was apparently covered with lots of smaller rocks. George and Dango, finding some the size of shot puts, proceeded to start shot-putting them from the summit to the ground below. They threw four or five off to the side of the party and none of the drinking crowd at the base even noticed. We were all having too much fun of our own.

But what was the point of shot-putting rocks if no one noticed? Dango and George decided to take a chance and drop a few near the keg to give us all a scare. That's what I mean about not knowing when to stop. George went first and put his stone off the boulder holding the keg. It hit with a "crack," then ricocheted off and slammed into someone's foot. A few of us around the keg looked up to see where the falling missile had originated. I looked up just as Dango's rock hit me in the head.

Friends told me later that when Dango found out I was the one bleeding from my head, out cold on the beer-soaked ground, he did jump down from the rocky promontory. All I remember is that I came to with Dango, Grabner and Lehmann, carrying me out of the woods to the road. A T-shirt was wrapped around my head and I could taste blood as it dripped down past my eyes and nose to my mouth. My head hurt like hell and, I could tell, my three friends carrying me were scared sober. They got me to Grabner's station wagon, put me in the back seat and rushed me to a small medical clinic in nearby Chagrin Falls.

The rock in the head was the exclamation point to the end of the summer of '62. I'm sure Lieutenant Gianelli would have said I was still lucky. And I was. By looking up the split second before the rock hit me, it landed on the front of my head above my left eye, and then glanced off. If I hadn't looked up, it would have hit, full force, squarely on top of my head and, most likely, cracked the skull. As it was, I ended up with a slight concussion and eight stitches. The scar ran from the top of my forehead back into my scalp. I can still feel it and see it sometimes to this day.

I stayed at Grabner's home in Shaker Heights for two nights and rested for the remainder of the weekend. Dango came to visit me every few hours it seemed. The pain and headaches had subsided by Monday. I returned to the sleeping hole in the morning to help Dango pack up our things. We were due to be out by Tuesday. Dango and John AuWerter were heading back to Rutgers on Wednesday. I figured I'd leave Cleveland and start driving back to California the same day.

It hardly took us any time to clean up our basement room. I only had to pack one large suitcase and a duffel. Dango threw all his clothes in a large trash bag to take home and throw in the wash. At noon, we walked down to our corner bar to get lunch. Hardly anyone was in there. We sat at the long bar and ordered our usual cheeseburger and fries. A couple of guys were in the back drinking beers and shooting some pool. About five stools down the bar, a drunk was passed out, his head resting on his folded hands on top of the bar next to an empty glass.

When the bartender brought over our draft beers, Dango clinked his glass to mine.

"Great summer, Lee!"

"Yeah, it was great," I said. "Thanks for everything, Bob."

"Even the head?"

"Yeah, even the head. Now I'll always have something to remember Dango and Cleveland."

The bartender brought the food. Dango and I, as was our custom whenever there was food, went silent. I looked down the bar at the passed-out gentleman whose face, even though flat on the bar with eyes closed, seemed to be looking at me. It hit me suddenly that I recognized him.

"Dango, I know that guy."

"The drunk?"

"He was my dentist. My mom took me to him back in elementary and junior high. Doc Reilly."

"Jesus! Better get your teeth checked when you get back to California."

We both laughed.

"You know," I said. "I'm going straight to Los Angeles. I'll be taking the exact route we took last year, only in reverse."

"Stop in Vegas and win some money. Skip Clovis," Dango replied as he finished the last of his burger.

After lunch we walked back to the sleeping hole for the last time to pick up our cars. We hugged awkwardly. Neither of us was much good at showing emotion.

"Next year," he said. "We'll do it again."

"Next year," I answered, "You're on."

Later that week, driving the Ghia back across country, I looked for one clean-cut hitchhiker to pick up. Maybe one with a sign that said "San Diego" or "Albuquerque," or "Student." I only had room for one rider in the small Ghia, but even though I saw hitchers, I never saw the one I wanted. There were certainly fewer with their thumbs out on the road then there had been in '61. Maybe it was because there were more miles of interstate completed.

I decided to follow Gianelli's advice and not "push it." I spent four nights staying in motels along the route. I made a slight detour to drive through Monument Valley. And I didn't stop in Las Vegas.

But Dango, heading toward Rutgers in the opposite direction from Cleveland, never stopped "pushing it."

CHAPTER 9

St. Louis to Columbus

We pulled into the city of St. Louis about 7:00 a.m. in Chuck's injured '57 Bel Air. He found an open Steak'N Shake for breakfast. We didn't have any Steak'N Shakes in Cleveland and you wouldn't think by the name it would be a good breakfast place, but Chuck swore by it. It was a landmark St. Louis restaurant chain, he said.Chuck called his girlfriend from the payphone and woke her up to come meet us. While we waited for her to get there I ordered breakfast. Steak and eggs, what else?

The last few miles of the drive into St. Louis had been uncomfortable. I sat in the back as far away from the "wire-hangered" door as I could. Chuck and Dango sat quietly in the front seat, each with their own thoughts. I knew what Dango was thinking about. In the heat of the moment after the crash, he'd promised to help Chuck pay for the damage. I knew he didn't have any money. I knew his parents weren't all that well off. They couldn't be going around paying for his mistakes. I also knew if his mom found out, not only would she make him pay for the car, she'd make him pay for the rest of his life.

While we were eating our steak and eggs, Chuck opened the negotiations.

"You said you could pay for the damages?" Chuck asked Dango.

Dango finished chewing a piece of steak, swallowed and answered, "I think I can help pay. I'll have to talk to my parents. I don't have the money myself."

"Can you call 'em from here?"

I could tell, the way Dango was concentrating on eating his food, that he was trying to figure out what to do.

The offer to help pay for the accident, made back in the foggy median of Route 66, was done hastily to move on from a bad situation. Now that we were safe and sound in St. Louis, Chuck expected Dango to make good on the words he had spoken.

Suddenly, Dango popped up from the booth.

"Hey, it's a little after seven here, that means it's a little after eight in Cleveland. My dad probably hasn't left for work yet. I'll call him."

I let him out of the booth and he headed for the payphone. He put in a dime and then I guess placed a collect call. He looked back over at Chuck and me after about a minute and gave us a thumbs-up.

"What's that mean?" Chuck asked me.

"Means his dad answered, not his mom."

Chuck watched Dango talking on the phone. I went back to my steak and eggs and ordered a chocolate milk shake to finish it off. I'd heard the shakes were great and, after all, it was part of the place's name. So what if it was 7:17 in the morning?

Dango came back to the table all smiles. He could be charming when he was trying to sell something.

"My dad says we'll be glad to help," he told Chuck.

I could literally see the tension in Chuck's body start to leave.

"Great," he said.

"Look, let's get some paper," Dango began. "We'll exchange phone numbers and addresses and when I get back to Cleveland . . ."

I started to tune out and concentrate on my shake, which was excellent by the way. Dango and Chuck were chatting away again, just as they had in the front of the Bel Air after we'd left Tulsa. Best buds. It didn't ring true to me. Dango was in conning mode. I knew and really liked Dango's father, Bob Lyons Sr. – Dango was a junior. But I knew him well enough to know he didn't say, "We'll be glad to help." He was a businessman and not prone to spending money when he didn't have to.

I also knew something else. Something my dad had told me very emphatically when he'd bought me the Star Chief.

"Lee, don't forget," he'd said. "If you let someone else, anyone else drive your car, you're responsible for anything that happens. That's why you don't let anyone drive your car, but you!"

I remembered that, which is why I'd driven the Pontiac even sometimes when it would have been wiser to let someone else drive. I also remembered that my dad had obtained an insurance rider on our policy for Dango when we drove to Sequoia.

I looked over at the two of them as they exchanged Steak'N Shake paper place-mats. They had just finished writing their personal information on the back. Then, they shook hands in the booth like they'd agreed on a business deal. Right after they shook, Chuck stood up.

"Here's Margy," he said, smiling.

Dango and I looked at the door as a young woman in khaki shorts entered. She saw Chuck and her face lit up. They quickly split the distance between door and booth to embrace and lock into a long kiss. After they broke their lovelock, Chuck brought her over to us.

"Margy, this is Bob and Lee."

"I'm glad all you guys are okay," she said as she shook our hands.

I think the best word in describing Margy would be "clean." She was about two inches shorter than Chuck, wore a button-down pink cotton shirt out over her shorts and, from what I could tell, almost no make-up. Her light brown hair was pulled back in a ponytail. The face wasn't what you would call beautiful, but attractive and open. She was like one of the Mouseketeers from the Mickey Mouse Club, only grown up. You immediately liked her. Chuck put his arm around her shoulder, and as they stood there facing us, I could imagine them in 10 years doing a family TV commercial for Steak'N Shake with their three kids.

"Look, we're going to take off," Chuck said. "Want us to drop you somewhere?"

Before I could say a word, Dango piped in, "No, we're great. You guys get outta here. We're fine. Thanks for everything."

We all hugged and shook hands and they were out the door. Margy followed Chuck in his beat-up Bel Air in her bright red, rear-engine Corvair as they exited the parking lot.

Dango and I turned to each other and, before I could ask him why he hadn't taken Chuck up on the offer to drop us at a good hitching place, he gave me the answer.

"Did I look good on the phone?" he said.

"You never called?" I asked, beginning to understand.

"Are you kidding? Tell my parents about this stuff? I'm on a Greyhound heading home. I'll figure something out when I get there. Let's get out of here."

I never asked Dango whether he ever contacted Chuck again. He told me once, because he knew it bothered me, that he and his father had talked to Chuck on the phone together. They never paid him anything.

It was because Dango wanted to be rid of Chuck as soon as he could that it took us a good two hours, walking and getting short rides, to get to the on-ramp for the bridge across the Mississippi. Another hour to get the ride to finally leave St. Louis and end up at the stop sign in the middle of East St. Louis, Illinois, where we hit a snag. It was noon on Friday August 4th, our fourth day out of Las Vegas. The sun was straight up, the temperature about 94°F and the humidity even higher. There was a large flat gravel area next to the road where Dango and I were hitchhiking. I don't call it a highway, because it was more of a detour between highways. Just after we crossed the Mississippi River from St. Louis, we ran into all kinds of road construction, where Route 66 went north heading on up through Illinois to Chicago and Highway 40 split off, heading east through the bottom part of the state to Indiana and Columbus, Ohio. Highway 40 was well on its way to becoming Interstate 70, which was the main reason for all the construction. North of where we were standing, we could make out the raised highway and unfinished steel and concrete overpasses under construction. The only traffic on it – skeletal caterpillar graders, giant bulldozers and dump trucks. That was going to be the 70 super highway of the future. For now, to connect to the soon-to-be-deceased 40, you had to zig and zag your way through East St. Louis.

Summer travelers were not happy campers to be strung-out on single lane roads, jammed in lines behind stop signs in the unbearable heat. What Dango and I thought was a great hitchhiking location – a spot by a stop sign right on the highway we wanted – had turned out to be a liability. Drivers were so furious and hot by the time they got to the stop sign, they gave us looks like we were responsible for the slow down. More than one young single driver, usually our best chance for a ride, had sneered at us and flipped us the bird just before they floored it and screeched away from the stop.

Dango and I alternated hitching because of the oppressive heat. One of us would stand smiling and looking presentable as he held his thumb out to the angry line of cars, the other would sit on one of the suitcases in a sliver of shade from a single tall tree off the highway and try to breathe and keep cool. When the hitcher could no longer hide his sweat and discomfort, we'd switch positions. We'd been there since 11:30 a.m. and expected to be gone in five minutes. Now we were hoping we'd be on the road before an hour passed.

It was during one of my hitchhiking stints in the brutal heat that an old gray-green '52 DeSoto pulled off onto the gravel before the stop sign. I saw the car was packed with a mom, dad and three kids, so I didn't give it a second thought. Probably one of the kids had to go pee off in the bushes or something. I went back to smiling and holding my thumb out to the other cars in the line.

Both passenger side doors opened. Three kids, two boys and one girl, ranging in age, I'd guess, from four to nine, got out and started running around. The oldest boy went over to Dango sitting in the sliver of shade. A thin woman in a very plain cotton dress stepped out of the front passenger seat and while leaning with her arms on top of the door, shouted to me.

"You boys want a ride?"

Instead of just jumping and saying, "Of course," I was so surprised I said, "Have you got enough room?"

"Wouldn't be asking if we didn't," she replied. "We're going right through Columbus."

The last thing I had done before we left Steak 'N Shake was take two backsides of the place-mats, tape 'em together, and make a "Columbus" sign to go with the "Students" sign. It was on the bag I was standing next to by the stop sign, facing the line of traffic. I looked over at Dango; he was standing now over by the other bags. He looked back at me and shrugged.

"Hey, if they want us, let's go."

The kids started jumping up and down with joy. I had a hunch they must have been bored stiff in the car and begged their parents to pick us up. The mother went back to open the trunk. The father just sat in the driver's seat and lit a cigarette. The older boy picked up our two small duffels, the girl and the youngest boy went to pick up Dango's bag. They both grabbed the handle and tried to lift it. The little boy's hand slipped off and he fell flat on his butt. The girl let out a grunt when she couldn't lift it.

"I'll get that one," said Dango, lifting it with his right hand.

He headed back to the trunk with his bag and I picked up mine and followed him. The mother was holding up the trunk when we got there and the boy had already put in our two duffels. I looked in the trunk; it was packed with bags, boxes and two other large duffels. I didn't see any room for our two suitcases.

"We'll get one more in here," the mom said. "And then put the other in the backseat."

She began to re-arrange things and then started to reach for Dango's bag.

"Better make it this one," Dango said, reaching over with his free hand to give her my bag. "I'll put mine in back."

She put my suitcase flat on top of all the other junk in the trunk and then slammed down the lid. I heard a loud click as the trunk lid shut. She gave it a try to make sure it had caught. I tried not to think about my suitcase as a pancake.

"Let's go," she said.

Dango put his suitcase in the floor space on the passenger side of the backseat. The older boy and girl climbed in on that same side with their feet on the seat. Dango sat in the middle next to his suitcase. I was next to him by the driver's side back window. The mom and the toddler sat up front.

The father, who hadn't said a word or even acknowledged we were in the car, flicked his cigarette out the window on to the gravel and edged back into the line of traffic. After we had passed the stop sign, Highway 40 opened up and we were quickly out of East St. Louis heading across the lower half of Illinois. There was no air conditioning in the old DeSoto; all the windows were open to catch the breeze on that midsummer scorcher of a day. The mother turned, put her arm up on the front seat and started with the introductions.

"We're the Kellers," she said. "My husband, Carl. I'm Sarah. The little one up here is Joshua, and back with you are David and Ruth."

As Dango made our introductions, I noted to myself that, except for the father, we were riding with a family of all biblical names. One look around the car and I was pretty sure we weren't traveling with the Rockefellers either. The two boys were dressed in just T-shirts and shorts, but the clothes had seen a lot of washing and drying in the sun – they were faded and dull. The girl wore a loose cotton print dress that had seen a few too many washes, too. The dullness in the wardrobe carried over to the car interior. Instead of vinyl seats, a worn gray fabric covered both front and back. There was a little chrome molding spotted here and there on the dash, but nothing like the amount of chrome you'd see in cars in the late '50s and early '60s. This was the low end DeSoto, whatever year it came out.

"So where'd you boys come from?" Sarah asked. "And where are you headed?"

"Well, we're headed home to Cleveland," Dango started off as he began to relate an embellished version of our travels. Sarah smiled. Little Joshua's head popped up over the back of the front seat and David and Ruth just gazed at Dango in rapture. You would have thought he was Tennessee Ernie Ford telling one of his country yarns on TV.

Every few minutes, Dango would be interrupted by one of the kids with a question like, "How big are the Sequoias?" or "You've seen the Pacific Ocean?" or "You've been to Las Vegas?" or "You saw oil wells?" Dango wouldn't skip a beat to add a few hundred feet to the trees, giant waves to the beach, hundreds of dollars to my jackpot and even a gusher to the oil wells. After about 20 minutes of sheer fantasy, he had to take a break to create something new.

I took the opportunity to ask Sarah where they were headed.

"We're going back home to family in Connecticut," Sarah said very matter-of-factly.

Before I could ask anything else she continued, "We had a small farm in Iowa, but couldn't make a go of it."

"It was a dream of mine," Carl said next, looking straight at the road ahead and never taking his hands off the wheel. "But without a lot of money, a small one-family farm is too hard. It's just a dream."

Sarah touched his shoulder with her hand that was on top of the seat. I saw Dango's eyes widen behind his big old horn-rimmed glasses. I was struck quiet. In just a few sentences a husband and wife had told us, two complete strangers, they had failed. I had never heard any of my friends' parents, my parents' friends, or anyone in the Heights, ever admit to failure. I didn't know how to respond.

I took this chance to look out the window at the passing scenery. You could tell we were in the Midwest. No vistas of empty space. Every five or six miles it seemed we'd pass through a small town. Between the towns, we'd see houses and farms, and row after row of crops. And people everywhere. Out west on Route 66, you could go for 100 miles without seeing a human being off the highway. On Route 40 through Southern Illinois every mile you'd see someone. In the towns, wood frame houses had large front yards that faced the highway. It seemed that every other yard had a big plastic circular pool, a hose spraying water and four or five kids escaping the heat and humidity of this August day.

"Anybody hungry?" Sarah said, breaking the silence. A chorus of shouted "I am!" from the kids made Sarah smile.

"Carl, next place you see that looks good, let's pull over for lunch."

Carl nodded. No change of expression, no taking his eyes off the road.

The next town we came to, Carl passed a Dairy Queen, a Stuckey's, an A&W root beer drive-through and a couple of other roadside stands without so much as slowing down. In the next town, he pulled over by a small roadside park with some old wooden picnic tables, a water fountain and small public bathrooms. Dango and I exchanged glances. We figured Sarah was going to be preparing lunch. Carl got out, stretched, touched his toes and then headed to the men's room. The children exited the car and began running, screaming and laughing. Sarah went to the back and opened the trunk.

"Can we help you?" Dango asked.

"Why, thank you," Sarah said. "If you'd take a few of these top bags off, I'll get what I need on the bottom."

I grabbed my suitcase, which had weathered the tight squeeze with only a rip in the "Columbus" sign. We wouldn't be needing that anymore, anyway. Dango took off some duffels and a couple of cardboard boxes filled with clothes. The trunk on the old square-shaped car was large and deep. Down at the bottom, Sarah removed a Styrofoam cooler and another cardboard box. She took the cooler to one of the tables. I carried over the box.

David and Ruth came over and grabbed Dango, one on each hand, and urged him to come play with them. Since they had found an oak tree partway up a small hill past the picnic tables, and since it offered the only shade in the park, Dango quickly followed them. I stood by the picnic table to help Sarah. I must admit I was curious to find out what kind of lunch was going to emerge from one cooler and cardboard box. Sarah opened the cooler and took out a new loaf of Wonder Bread. Then she reached in and removed a large jar of strawberry jam and one of peanut butter. Both the jam and peanut butter were about three-quarters full. There were a few other things in there. I saw a quart of milk, but I couldn't see what else, because she closed the lid quickly. Everything was nice and chilled, so I'm betting she had a chunk of dry ice on the bottom. She then opened the box.

I had carried the box over to the table and it wasn't that heavy, but I was amazed at all she took out of it. First out was a small, red-and-white checkered plastic tablecloth. She spread that on the table and then she pulled out two stainless steel table knifes, six plastic Melmac plates, six paper napkins and six paper cups. To finish, she reached in and came out with a two-quart plastic pitcher that was probably aqua in color at one time, but now was translucent from repeated use and cleanings. I just stood there waiting for her to pull the rabbit out next. Instead of a rabbit, she handed me the pitcher.

"Lee, could you fill that at the water fountain, please, while I prepare the sandwiches?"

As I walked over to the water fountain, she removed a couple of other things from the miracle box and then put the box and cooler under the table in the shade. The water from the fountain was refreshingly cool, almost cold – it must have come straight from an underground spring. I took a quick swig before filling the pitcher and noticed that Carl had come out of the men's room. He had lit another cigarette and stood watching Dango and the kids playing on the hill. He was dressed in lace-up work boots, army green work pants and a gray T-shirt. His face was tan, thin and chiseled. He had close-cropped, almost a crew cut, salt and pepper hair. "Hard" just kept coming to mind every time I watched him. Life had treated him hard. He was not going to break, he was just going to get harder.

When I took the full pitcher of water back to the table, Sarah was screwing the lid back on the peanut butter. 12 slices of Wonder Bread had been paired off on the tablecloth; one of each pair had been spread with peanut butter. Sarah handed me two packets of cherry Kool-Aid and the top to the pitcher.

"Lee, can you mix the Kool-Aid? I need to spread the jam quickly before the peanut butter melts."

"Glad to," I said.

I emptied the two packets in the water, put on the top and carefully shook the pitcher to mix the bright red brew. Sarah quickly spread the jam and closed the sandwiches.

"Come on everyone," she shouted. "Lunch is ready." The kids ran down from the hill, pulling Dango along. Carl walked over and stood by Sarah. No one reached or grabbed for their sandwich. When everyone was standing around the table, Sarah took Carl's hand in her right hand and little Joshua's hand in her left. Joshua reached over and grabbed David's, who took Dango's, who took Ruth's, who took mine, and when I reached out to take Carl's the circle was closed. Dango and I caught each other's eye just before Sarah said grace. I think we were both surprised at how automatically we had known what was coming. Everyone bowed their heads.

"God bless this food we are about to receive. Amen," Sarah said.

Soon as she was done, the kids grabbed their peanut butter and jellies. Dango and I waited a beat and took ours. Sarah and Carl took the last two.

"Lee, would you please pour everyone a cup of Kool-Aid?" Sarah asked.

I picked up the full pitcher I had just mixed and proceeded to fill the six waiting cups. Once again, the kids grabbed theirs first, and took their sandwiches and drinks up the hill to the shade of the tree. Dango followed them. I sat on one of the table benches to devour my lunch. Talk about "comfort food" – a peanut butter and jelly sandwich on Wonder Bread, not toasted, is about as comfortable as you can get. It's so soft you really don't need any teeth to chew it. Wonder Bread, in those days, used to advertise how healthy it was. Of course, cigarettes in '61 were advertised in all the magazines and comic book back covers with puffing Major League baseball players, too. Whether the Wonder Bread was healthy or not didn't make any difference to any of us on that hot August day. It was easy and good to eat and all gone in about two minutes. The semi-cool Kool-Aid was too sweet for me. I tipped out half my cup when no one was looking.

Carl had another cigarette with his lunch and then lay down on the slope of the hill and covered his face with an old beat-up baseball cap. I helped Sarah clean up the few items left from lunch at the drinking fountain. She rinsed off the peanut butter knife and handed it to me to dry with a small dish towel I was holding.

"Carl has the ability to fall asleep instantly when he needs to get rest," she said. "We'll let him sleep about 20 minutes before we leave."

I handed her back the dry peanut butter knife and she gave me the wet jelly knife.

"Can I ask you a question?" I said.

"Certainly."

"Why did you pick us up?"

"You needed a ride," Sarah said. "We could give you a ride."

I helped her complete the few chores at the table to pack the box and cooler, and then went up the hill to join Dango and the kids. Sarah busied herself repacking the trunk and cleaning the inside of the DeSoto.

Dango and the three children were so intent on playing some game they'd made up, I don't think they even noticed me when I sat down with my back to the tree trunk.

From what I could make out, it was some kind of battle royal going on. Dango had to stay on his knees to make it fair. His job was to protect little Joshua from the clutches of his evil siblings. David and Ruth would dart and dance around Dango, trying to grab Joshua. Dango would reach out with his long arms and push them gently or hold them and tickle them for an instant. The laughter, giggling and shouting was incessant. Little Joshua was crying from how much fun he was having. A couple of times David and Ruth would charge Dango, jump on him, and all four would roll partway down the hill, Dango carefully making sure not to put his weight on top of anyone.

As I watched from my perch under the tree, I couldn't help but be struck by how quickly the kids had bonded to my big best friend. It's not that it was surprising, in fact – just the opposite. The kids loved him just the way his friends loved him, the way the guys at the warehouse loved him, or the way the guys in the tree crew loved him – because he loved all of them, unconditionally. That's not easy to do. I know I couldn't do it. I know there were kids at University School that didn't like me, because they thought I was phony or scheming. Hell, I was phony and scheming with most everyone, except for Dango. I tried to think at that moment of anyone who knew Dango who didn't like him. I couldn't think of anyone. His openness and honesty, coupled with his "in 20 years" devil-may-care attitude made him irresistible, and I smiled as I watched him playing with the kids on that Southern Illinois hillside, because I realized that he would make a wonderful father someday.

But maybe there was one person who didn't like Dango – I don't think Dango liked himself much after he'd had too many beers.

On a cold December morning about a week before Christmas break in 1962, John AuWerter woke up at 1:45 a.m. in his Demarest dormitory room at Rutgers University. He had to pee bad. As he put on the bomber jacket thrown at the foot of his bed, he checked the bed next to his. Dango, his roommate, was not there. Since their beds were always a mess, he could not tell whether he'd slept in it at all that night. Stumbling to the door, he remembered what they'd done last night. They had spent the first hour after dinner actually studying in their room. Dango had an accounting test on Friday, so papers were still scattered on his small desk with columns and columns of numbers. Dango was good at accounting, always precise and accurate, but he hated it. John had been reading for his English class: Restoration poetry.

At about 8:00 p.m., they'd heard a shout from down the hall: "Keg! Room 107." It was not an unusual occurrence to have kegs in Demarest. Probably two or three times a month, some dorm mate would have something to celebrate. Since dorms had their own prefects and governing councils, they made their own rules. The rule at Demarest about having a keg in your room was - it had to be shared. Free beer quickly beat out accounting and poetry with Dango and John. They were conveniently located on the ground floor in Room 102, only two doors from the front door and just five away from Room 107. They picked up their Rutgers' mugs and went down to join the group. After two mugs and 15 minutes, John and Dango made an attempt to go back to their room and continue studying. That lasted about half an hour. A little after 9:00 p.m., they returned to 107 to have some more beer and horsing around before they hit the sack. At 11:15 John had had enough, so he headed back to 102. Dango, feeling no pain, and not having had enough beer or fun, told John he'd see him in the morning.

That was what John recalled of the evening as he headed for the bathroom at the end of the hall at 1:45 p.m. to get rid of some of those earlier beers. Walking down the hall, John was surprised to see three or four other students and two policemen gathered outside the bathroom. One of the students started walking toward him in the opposite direction. Just as he was passing he turned to

John and said, "Bathroom's closed."

John continued to walk down to the group and saw one of his buddies from earlier in 107.

"What happened?" John asked.

"Dango," the friend responded.

What really "happened," no one will ever know, because no one was there when it happened – except for Dango.

John walked up to the bathroom door that was opened but cordoned off with yellow crime scene tape, and looked in. It looked like a bomb had gone off. The debris on the floor caught John's eye first: shattered pieces of porcelain in all sizes; two wooden privy stall doors ripped apart with their hinges still attached; huge chunks of granite from the privy divider walls; sharp, jagged pieces of glass from the mirrors over the sinks; water running around and through all the various debris to a small drain in the center of the floor. To top off the devastation strewn around the floor, three or four college-boy-sized stools bumped and floated about. The stench, never good in a college men's dormitory bathroom, was nauseating. Thank goodness the drain in the center of the floor was still open. Thank goodness it was the middle of winter, not the middle of summer, when heat would only have added to the stink and brought the insects.

John lifted his eyes from the floor to view the damage: Three out of five sinks were sheared off to pedestal stumps. Two out of five mirrors were obliterated – only 14 years' bad luck. Three granite privy walls destroyed. Three toilet tanks ripped off and shattered, water flowing out of them. Two toilet bowls turned into half-bowls. One wooden privy door yanked partway off, with a splintered hole in it, hanging on one hinge to go with the other two doors on the floor. There was no damage to the urinals. The back window was shattered and wide open, letting in the freezing air. A policeman in a heavy, blue, knee-length jacket and rubber winter boots was walking very carefully around the destruction. He wrote notes on a clipboard he held in his hands. John assumed it was to catalog the damage.

Suddenly, a large drop of water landed on the clipboard, startling the policeman. He looked up. John followed his gaze and saw that the bathroom had become some kind of biology room environmental experiment – a terrarium from hell. The frigid air from the blown out window had mixed with the air from the heated bathroom to create a gray rain cloud that seemed to be clinging to the ceiling. Small points of fog would form below the cloud to drop their pellets of water then recede back into the cloud to reappear somewhere else. The one overhead frosted light dome, still on, cast an eerie glow through the cloud.

John pulled back from the door. He felt like he had to throw up. He ran back to room 102, crossed over Dango's empty bed and opened the window. He leaned out and chucked up what was left of his dinner mixed with beer. Then he reached down, pointed his pecker out the open window and emptied his bladder, thus completing the chore that had awoken him in the first place. He quickly closed the window to shut out the smell and cold. He then turned and looked back at the small, messy Rutgers' dorm room and to no one in particular said, "Dango, what have you done?!"

What he had done was obvious; how exactly he had done it or why he had done it, no one would ever discover. There were no witnesses to the act. Dango was found standing on top of a parked pizza delivery truck and arrested by the Rutgers Police at 12:53 a.m. Maybe the pizza delivery guy had made a late call to one of the dorms and come out after dropping off a large pepperoni to find Dango there and called the cops. He would have immediately known something was wrong; Dango was only wearing his Air Force bomber jacket – no pants, no shoes – and holding a large piece of the privy granite in both his hands. The rage must have left somewhere between the blown-out bathroom window and the truck top. He offered no resistance to the police and went quietly to jail. Maybe it dawned on him his legs and feet were freezing.

Rutgers wasted no time in expelling him. Dango's parents were called and his father drove down from Cleveland the next day. Dango was released to his father's custody. John helped them pack up his things at dinnertime and load them into his dad's

Ford station wagon. It was already dark. Dango's father drove the Ford because he had to follow Dango as he rode his Triumph 650 motorcycle back home. Just as Dango had told Ron and Joanna he would over a year and a half earlier, he had gotten his Triumph. He had used the money he earned from the tree service work to buy it.

As for the "bathroom incident," as it came to be known in the old boys' University School circle, it was never talked about much. When it was, it was "Crazy Dango," or "Dango's Drunken Rampage," or "Dango's Rutgers' re-decorating." I heard about it in a postcard he sent me from Cleveland to Claremont. He said he didn't remember it at all and checked it off to college drunkenness. I had a moment of concern when I read it, then shook it off. I was 19, twenty-five hundred miles away and never realized the degree of violence and destruction. I was not alone. No one else saw it as a "red flag" or a "call for help", either.

"Lee, come on!" Dango shouted.

Despite the screaming kids, I had dozed off in the shade of the tree on the hill. I stood up and looked down to see the Keller family and Dango looking up at me, ready to get back on the road. Carl was already in the driver's seat finishing a new cigarette. I jogged down to join them and everybody re-claimed their assigned seats. I checked my watch; it was 2:48 p.m. We had over 170 miles to go before we got to Columbus.

It only took about 15 minutes for the heat, the motion of the car and the digesting food to hit the kids: David and Ruth were sound asleep, each with a head on Dango's shoulder. Joshua was sleeping in Sarah's lap. Dango looked over at me with his big grin and raised his eyebrow with the same "What can I do?" look he'd given me when he was in the back seat with Joanna. This time I could smile back.

I could tell he didn't want to move and disturb the kids, so instead he just put his head back and in a couple of miles he was out, too. Sarah had her head resting on the back of the front seat facing Carl; I watched as her eyes closed. Once again, I was in a car full of sleeping people. I looked at the back of Carl's head directly in front of me. No nodding whatsoever, he sat ramrod straight, both hands on the wheel, the left arm leaning on the driver's side open window. I thought about asking him if he needed a break, but the more I thought about it, I knew it would be a mistake. He was determined to drive his family where they had to go; he would never let someone he picked up help him – that would be weakness.

I was so sure of this, I decided to try and get a little more rest. I closed my eyes, leaned back and let the warm breeze from the open window blow over me. I listened to the sound of the tires on the road and sounds of traffic and towns as we passed – but I couldn't sleep. After two accidents caused by falling asleep in cars my mind refused to turn off. I opened my eyes and watched the scenery as we passed through Southern Illinois and Central Indiana.

This was the middle of Middle America and I thought, as we passed through, that there was nothing extraordinary about it. The one traffic light towns all looked pretty much the same and most of them had all-American names like Casey, Marshall, Cloverdale and Plainfield. Terre Haute recalled a little bit of America's French heritage, but the section of town we passed through didn't look any different than Marshall or Plainfield. Lots of pick-up trucks and Chevrolets, and billboards with smiling people enjoying their Cokes next to the giant bright red Coke logo button. Everywhere you looked people were outside enjoying their summer in shorts and light cotton dresses. And they were all white people – on the billboards, in the trucks and on the streets. As the sophisticated Heights' boy passing through, it seemed pretty boring. Years later, recalling the trip, it would seem extraordinary – like another country.

The only real town of any size we passed through was Indianapolis. Highway 40 went right through the center of town and the lights and traffic slowed us down quite a bit. As we headed out of Indianapolis to the east, Carl saw something that made him wake the entire car.

"Hey everybody, look over to your left up here."

I looked to my left and saw a gigantic parking lot and, off in the distance, a stadium of some kind. I knew Indianapolis didn't have a major league football or baseball team so I was wondering what the big deal was. And then I saw a large oval sign at the main entrance to the parking lot.

"Home of the Indianapolis 500"

"The Most Famous Car Race in the World!"

"It's the Indy Brickyard, David," Carl exclaimed. "They race at speeds over 100 miles an hour."

"Can we take a look, Dad? Is that where A.J. won?" David asked.

"Nah. Nothing's happening now. The race is at the beginning of every summer, on Memorial Day. But that's where A.J. won it."

It came back to me then that a guy named A.J. Foyt had won the Indy 500 in May. It was the first time he'd won. He'd go on to win two more times in the '60s and once more in 1977 – one of the few four-time winners ever. Indy car racing wasn't big with teenagers from US or the Heights.

"Have you guys ever seen an Indy car race?" David asked me and Dango.

"Nope. I'm not a big sports fan kinda guy," Dango admitted. "But Lee goes to see the Cleveland Browns and Cleveland Indians."

"You seen Jim Brown in person?" David asked me.

"Not to shake his hand," I replied. "But I've seen him run. I went to one game where he disappeared into the line, then came out the other side and scored a touchdown."

"Wow!" David said, impressed.

Little Joshua's head appeared over the back of the front seat and he looked at me with the same expression of awe I'd just received from David. Ruth seemed to be glad to just hear me talk. I decided I liked the attention Dango had been getting, so I continued.

"My dad and I try to go to as many Yankees-Indians games as we can."

"You seen Mickey Mantle in person?"

"Sure did. I was at one game where he hit one home run left-handed and then one right-handed."

"No!"

"Yup. And I was at the game where Gil McDougald nailed Herb Score."

"Who's Herb Score?"

I started to explain how Herb Score was well on his way to becoming the next Bob Feller for the Indians, when Gil McDougald of the Yankees lined one of his 100mph fast balls back into his eye and basically ended his career when I noticed I was losing my audience. I went back to talking about Mantle and his current home run race with teammate Roger Maris to re-spark the kids' interest.

"Do you think he'll break Babe's record?" David said, talking about Mantle.

No one during that year ever really talked about Maris's chances until September.

"I hope so," I said.

And I did hope so, like so many teenage fans of that era. There was something about Mickey, the most magnificent athlete ever to swing a bat that you had to love. He had a great smile, could hit a ball 500 feet and fielded with grace and speed, but all that talent wasn't why you loved him. You loved him for the ways he was like you. He was far from perfect. He played in pain every day from bum legs. He drank and partied too much and played through hangovers. And most important to all of us, he didn't take himself too seriously. Dango and I knew he would have understood our "in

20 years" credo and approved.

The kids started to doze off again after my brief sports' highlights. The monotony of the constant travel began to wear on them. About an hour after Indianapolis, they were all asleep again when we crossed into Ohio. Dango and I couldn't sleep now; we were on the home stretch. Our main concern was to get to Columbus and catch a ride to Cleveland before dark. Carl sat like a statue driving; the only time he took a hand off the wheel was to light a new cigarette. Except for the slowdowns through towns, he kept the old DeSoto exactly on 60 – never more, never less. Dango and I figured the last leg in Ohio to be about two hours. We entered Ohio at 5:00 p.m., and thought we should hit Columbus by 7:00. That would give us 2 hours more of daylight to get a night ride to Cleveland. Hell, with luck, we could be home before midnight.

Time crawled those last miles to Columbus. We couldn't talk much for fear of waking the family. Dango couldn't move much with David and Ruth sleeping against him. The two of us sat together in the back seat and communicated with facial expressions, whispers and hand signs. Most of the looks were raised eyebrows and sneers of frustration at the slow passage of miles.

When we saw the first mileage sign to Columbus at under 30 miles, Dango nudged me and whispered: "Get my wallet out of my back pocket."

He leaned forward as much as he could without disturbing the sleeping youngsters and I reached behind and removed his wallet. I put it on top of his left leg. We had left Las Vegas with about $72 or so each and both of us had about $40 left. Not too bad for covering 2500 miles. Dango reached into his wallet and took out a $20. He folded it to the size of a stick of gum and squinched it into the crack between the seat and back cushion. Not totally hidden, but something you wouldn't see at first glance.

"I'm leaving this," he whispered.

I knew immediately what he was doing, why he was doing it and why he was semi-hiding it. If I hadn't been 18, I probably would have cried. As it was, I wanted to lean over and kiss him, but since I couldn't do that either, I just reached into my back pocket, took out my wallet and followed suit.

At 7:22 p.m., the DeSoto heading east on Highway 40 crossed over the new Interstate 71 in Columbus – to the northeast it went to Cleveland, heading southwest it reached Cincinnati. Carl pulled over at the first parking spot he could find. Everyone got out to say goodbye and help us get our bags on to the sidewalk.

The kids were strangely quiet and Joshua stayed in Sarah's arms. We gave them all hugs. Carl stayed by the driver's door and shook our hands. They all got back in the car and drove off. We could see David and Ruth in the back window waving to us as the DeSoto got smaller heading east.

We picked up our bags, crossed the street and walked back half a block, right up to the on-ramp to Interstate 71. The green sign above our heads had the following in large white letters with an arrow pointing north: "Cleveland – 144 miles."

CHAPTER 10

Columbus to Cleveland

"We're home free," Dango said.

The minute he said it, I knew he shouldn't have. So, right away, I asked what he meant.

"Only 144 miles to go. Two more hours of daylight. We'll be home by 11. Hell, we could call the guys and see what's going on tonight."

That's what I was afraid he meant. It was true that in the past 36 hours, we had managed to cross almost half the country. Even with a car wreck and the delay getting out of St. Louis, we had gone from Clovis, New Mexico to Columbus, Ohio faster than if we'd been on a Greyhound. But what Dango didn't understand, never understood, was that when you're in a run of good luck, you never talk about it. Just when I was about to tell him that, a two-door Ford Fairlane with a single guy pulled over and stopped.

"Where 'ya headed?" he shouted across the front seat through the open passenger window to Dango.

"Cleveland," Dango shot back.

"Oh, I'm going up three exits, if you want a lift that far?" he said.

"No," Dango answered, without skipping a beat, or getting my opinion. "Thanks anyway."

"How do you know that three exits up won't be a better spot than here?" I asked.

"Hey, this is where Highway 40 crosses 71. Someone's gonna be going all the way to Cleveland. Someone's gonna pick us up."

"Hope you're right," I said. "But I think I'll run into one of these stores here and see if I can't make us a 'Cleveland' sign."

"No, no," Dango said. "Not enough time. We've only got about two hours of daylight left; we'll get a ride soon. I feel lucky."

Boy, I shuddered when I heard that comment. He'd felt lucky in Vegas, too.

In the next half-hour, we had about three other cars stop. Not one of them was going all the way to Cleveland. Not even close. After an hour, the sun was right on the western horizon and we decided we'd take the next ride no matter where it took us to break our run of "good luck." I was thumbing when a young couple in a pick-up stopped. They were heading up 9 exits to one of the last northern suburbs of Columbus. We decided to chance it after the girl said: "If anyone gets onto 71 North from there, they're probably headed to Cleveland." We piled in back and in about 15 minutes we were standing by another on-ramp where the sign read "Cleveland – 130 miles".

After about 10 minutes at this new location, Dango's optimism finally turned to pessimism. I, of course, had been pessimistic since I'd heard him utter "We're home free." Not that I think the girl lied to us; it was just that no one turned onto 71 North from wherever the hell we were. Only two semis and two cars had entered the on-ramp and none of them had slowed for a second. At 9:30, in the half-light of dusk, a green vapor light turned on far above our heads. We could see all these strange green lights turn on at each on-ramp and off-ramp up and down the highway.

"At least we're illuminated," Dango said turning to me.

I looked back at him and it wasn't too dark to see that he was wearing that big grin. It was a joke and he was letting me know that he'd been way too "bully-bully" and he knew it.

At 10:30, neither of us was laughing. Except for the glow from the green overhead light, it was pitch black and we hadn't moved an inch. What really angered us was looking up onto 71 and seeing quite a bit of traffic whizzing by at 70 miles per hour – half of 'em had to be headed all the way to Cleveland.

At about 10:35, an empty flatbed stake truck with a man driving stopped in the pool of green light.

"I don't know if it'll help you," he said. "But I'm going up about 20 miles to Route 37."

Dango didn't waste a beat and started throwing our bags in the back of the truck.

"Thanks a lot," he said. "It's got to be better than here."

I swear to god, he couldn't help himself. In hitchhiking, you never know whether the next place you're dropped off is going to be better or worse than the last place. But you can be sure it'll always be worse if you jinx it by saying out loud that it's going to be better.

Twenty miles and 30 minutes later, Dango and I were standing by the Cleveland bound on-ramp from Route 37 to Interstate 71. The farmer who had driven us here said 37 got some cross-state traffic, but I know for a fact it didn't get any traffic after 11:00 p.m. It didn't even rate one of those weird green vapor lights on the on-ramp entrance. They were all up on 71 now to illuminate the ramps and overpasses. The traffic on 71 had started to thin out, too. Every few minutes you'd hear a big semi approach and then see it flash by overhead. Even the occasional cars would snap by at what seemed like 80-plus miles-per-hour. I timed it, and not one car even came down Route 37 in 20 minutes. It started to get cold for an August evening. A tulle fog began to build. I took my light jacket out of my bag, put it on and began to look at the brush off the side of the road to see if I could find a spot where we could lie down. It was 11:38.

At 11:40, Dango said, "Let's go up on 71."

"It's against the law to hitchhike on the interstate," I said.

"It's against the law for us to drink beer. It's the only way we'll ever get a ride."

"Bob, at this hour, the odds are better we'll catch a Highway Patrol car than a ride."

"So what?" he said. "I'd rather sleep in jail then spend the night out here."

With that he picked up his bags, crossed deserted Route 37 and headed up the off-ramp to Interstate 71. He had a point. I picked up my bags and followed him. But, to save some face, I shouted ahead to him: "Okay, but set a limit."

"Whatta ya mean?"

"We give it up after twenty cars, or twenty minutes."

"Thirty cars or thirty minutes," he countered.

"Deal," I said, figuring we'd be lucky to see 30 cars in two hours the way the traffic had thinned out.

We positioned ourselves about 30 feet in front of the Route 37 off-ramp under one of the green vapor lights. With the strange light and the building fog, we must have looked like diaphanous ghosts when we suddenly appeared to drivers barreling north at over 70 miles per hour. At 11:45 Dango first put out his thumb to a set of headlights heading toward us. A large semi rushed by in the lane closest to us and, just to be an asshole, set off his air horn. Dango and I jumped back.

"Doesn't count," Dango said, referring to our limit. "Wasn't a car."

There were hardly any cars heading north that late on a Friday night; maybe one for every three trucks. And the cars we did see, we only saw for a second. It seemed every car driver was going 80 to get in as many miles as he could before the fog really socked in and forced traffic to slow down. The lights would appear out of the fog and, by the time we got our thumbs up, they'd be by us. No one even slowed down. On the positive side, maybe the fog was keeping the Highway Patrol at home. Never saw one. Big negative – five more giant semis waited 'til they were right on top of us to hit their air horns. Friday night entertainment for the teamsters.

The eighth car came out of the fog like all the other cars – had to be going well over 70 and passed us in a blur. I knew it was the eighth car because I was the one counting. We were going to hit the time limit before the car limit; it was now 12:05 a.m. Dango and I lowered our thumbs and, just as we did, we heard the kind of god-awful screeching of tires you hear before there's a crash and a terrible accident. We looked back to the north at the car that had passed. We saw the taillights through the fog fishtailing back and forth across the two lanes of 71 and then come to a stop under another green ghost light by the side of the interstate, just past the bridge crossing Route 37.

Dango picked up his bags and started walking toward the car. "I think they've stopped for us."

"You sure?" I said. "Maybe they just missed their exit."

I started following Dango though; the car was a good football field away. As we got closer, we hesitated a bit. The car was a similar shape to the Keller's DeSoto, but not in as nice condition. It was black, but with a few patches that shone white in the strange light where somebody had used cheap body repair patch. I figured it to be a Plymouth – same early '50s vintage as the DeSoto, same Chrysler family. What made us hesitate was that the car hadn't moved since we'd started walking. The lights were still on, the motor running, windows closed, not a sign of life.

"Dango, hold up." I shouted.

I caught up to him and we put our bags down for a second.

"Maybe something's wrong." I said.

That's all it took. Right after I said it, the driver's side window rolled down. A giant black arm about the size of one of my legs appeared and waved us forward.

"Come on!" a voice boomed.

Dango and I looked at each other; this time we both smiled, this time we both said it without saying it: "What the hell!"

We picked up our bags and headed to the car. It was an old Plymouth. When we were a few feet from the trunk, both front doors opened and two of the largest black men I had ever seen emerged into the foggy night. Dango and I stopped again and just stared. The driver had to be about 6'4", close-cropped hair, giant arms as I've already mentioned; he was wearing dark slacks, a light blue, short-sleeved, buttoned shirt, not tucked in. His skin color was black black. I would have pegged him for an interior lineman on the Browns because of his build, except for the fact that even with the shirt out you could tell he had a little paunch. The passenger was only an inch or so shorter, his skin a couple of shades lighter, and he was wearing jeans. He didn't have a belly; he could have been a linebacker.

They started walking toward us. The passenger opened the trunk and the driver said, "We're goin' to Cleveland. You comin'?"

He said it with one of the biggest damn smiles you could imagine, because I was sure he knew the effect he was having on the two Heights boys. I guess I should just talk for this white boy, because I never knew how scared Dango had been, but I'd been ready to pee my pants 'til I saw that smile.

"You bet," Dango said, and handed his bag to the linebacker by the open trunk.

The muscle bound shotgun rider took it from Dango and immediately dropped it to the road.

"Shiiiit!" he said, looking at Dango funny, "What the hell you got in that bag, man?"

"Weights," Dango answered.

"You fuckin' nuts, bro," he said, laughing as he spoke. "RJ, pick up that bag. See what that boy's carrying."

The driver reached over and picked up Dango's bag with one arm, hefted it a few times then put it in the trunk.

"You are nuts, boy."

Then he looked at me and put his large hand out for my bag.

"You carrying weights, too?" he said. "Cause if you is, we'll just leave your bag here."

"No sir," I said, handing him my suitcase.

"That's for sure," he said as he flipped my bag into the trunk and closed the lid. "Let's go, time's a-wasting."

With that, they both headed to their respective sides, opened the doors and hopped in. Dango and I opened the two back doors, threw our duffels in the space between us and jumped in the backseat. RJ didn't waste a second to start to pull back onto 71. Fortunately, he didn't pull all the way into the lane, because a semi hit his air horn and almost scraped the paint off the Plymouth as it blew by.

"Fuckin' teamsters," RJ said, as he checked his mirror this time and merged into the lane.

"Been doing it to us all night," Dango said.

"My name's Randell Jackson," the driver said, as the Plymouth reached its cruising speed of about 68 mph. "But everyone calls me RJ. This here is Jerry Harris."

"That's me," said the giant in the shotgun seat. "But call me Jere."

"I'm Lee," I replied. "And this is Bob, but everybody calls him Dango."

"Dango!?" RJ said. "Where'd you get that name?"

Dango began to explain it and that got the conversation and the ride off to a nice smooth start. It wasn't long before Jere reached between his legs to the floor and pulled up a half empty, half-gallon bottle of some cheap wine. He took a swig and passed it back to Dango.

"You boys want a taste? Come on boys, the weekend's just starting."

"Sure thing," Dango said as he took the bottle and chugged a little.

He passed it to me and I lifted it to my lips when the smell hit me. This was Thunderbird or some other rotgut cheap wine they could sell over the counter in Ohio. That meant it had to be under 5%

alcohol content; anything over 5% had to be purchased in a state liquor store. No way I was going to refuse the offer, though; so I pretended to drink but kept my lips closed. The little I tasted with my tongue almost made me gag. I passed the bottle back to Jere, who gave it to RJ. He took it in his right hand and somehow the half-gallon didn't look much larger than a Coke bottle as he took his sizable quaff.

"How come you going up to Cleveland so late?" Dango asked.

"Poontang," RJ said. "We got ourselves some nice young ladies up in Cleveland, don't we, Jere?"

"Cleveland's the place, man," Jere continued. "Nothin' happens in Columbus on weekends. Minute we got off our shifts, we headed north."

"You guys been to Gleason's?" I asked.

"Gleason's! You white boys been to Gleason's?!" RJ said excitedly. "That's the best damn club in the state."

And with that the ride and the conversation kept getting better. The two big black guys, probably in their late 20s, and the two white Heights' boys, still in their teens, loved all the same things – good black music, hot women, something to drink and Cleveland on the weekends. Watch out Cleveland, we were on our way home and having a blast getting there.

First sign of any trouble was when RJ slowed the Plymouth down and said, "Damn, this fog is getting worse."

We all looked outside. A solid gray mist surrounded the car. The headlights made the fog in front of the Plymouth white and you could only make out about five feet of interstate pavement ahead of you. RJ cut the speed to about 45mph and switched from high beams to low. I guess, in a way, it was kind of lucky the fog slowed us down, because a few minutes later there was a loud 'Bang!'.

"Shiiit," Jere said. "Blow out."

The car started to limp along leaning to the right, "ka-thump, ka-thump, ka-thump." The right rear had blown. RJ pulled off to the right shoulder, put the Plymouth in park and left the engine running and the lights on.

"We got a spare?" he said, turning to Jere.

"Oh yeah, we got a couple of spares," Jere said. "That ain't the problem."

"What's the problem?" RJ asked.

Jere didn't answer, but opened the passenger door and walked back to the trunk. RJ followed him. Out of curiosity, and not wanting to look like spoiled white boys sitting in the back waiting on their drivers, we got out, too.

Jere had opened the trunk already, thrown my bag to the pavement and was lifting Dango's out when we got there.

"That's the problem," he said, nodding to what remained in the trunk.

Our bags had actually been resting on a bed of loose tires. I'd guess there were about four or five. The "problem" was that none of the tires were on a rim. Jere moved the tires a bit to reveal two empty rims on the floor of the trunk beneath the tires.

"That's no good," said RJ.

I had been expecting RJ, who I assumed was the leader of the pair, to blow his stack, but he just nodded like he was thinking and said, "That's no good." again. Not mad or anything.

"So we got a jack and wrench and everything?" he asked Jere.

"Nope, none of that either."

"Well we best get going and see if we can find someone to help us," RJ said as he headed back to the driver's seat. Jere followed this time. Dango and I put our bags back in the trunk, shut the lid and went back to our seats – all the time looking at each other with expressions that said: "What the hell just happened?"

To this day, I still don't get it. Why was it Jere's responsibility to get the spare? Or was it? How do you prepare for a flat tire by getting four spares and two rims, and not putting one of the spares on one of the rims? You just didn't get around to it? Whose car was it anyway? Maybe it belonged to both of them? I'll never know the answers but it gave Dango and I another cockeyed story for the end of our cross-country journey.

Back in the Plymouth, RJ slowly edged the crippled car back onto foggy 71. In a way, the fog was our best friend now. It was so thick no one was speeding along at much over forty. So when cars and trucks came up behind the tilting Plymouth struggling along at about 20 mph, they had time to see us and space to pass safely. Some of the semis that passed gave us their air horn salutes again. The few cars that came up on us quickly moved to the left lane and blew by. No one stopped to offer us a hand.

After a few miles of the steady "ka-thumping" you could start to smell rubber and hear and feel metal on the road. The right rear tire was steadily shredding as the rim now rolled along 71. Here we were on a brand new interstate and the ride was worse than our half day in the boxcar without suspension. I thought RJ's and Jere's mood would begin to darken, but nothing was going to dampen their enthusiasm for a weekend in Cleveland. They kept passing the jug of lousy wine, telling stories about what fun they were going to have, and laughing. Dango and I sat back, relaxed, enjoyed the show and got used to the grinding, uncomfortable ride.

It wasn't too long before we spotted a car, through the fog, parked off on the right shoulder. It had its parking lights on to make it somewhat visible to the passing traffic. Jere saw it as an opportunity.

"Hey RJ, maybe they got a spare and a jack we can use?"

That suggestion was enough for RJ. He pulled the Plymouth over to the shoulder a few feet behind the car and stopped. It was a '60 or '61 Oldsmobile sedan, and besides the taillights, there was no other sign of life.

"Why don't you go see," RJ said to Jere.

Jere got out and started walking slowly up to the car. The entire scene was illuminated in the Plymouth's headlights. Nothing stirred in the Oldsmobile. Dango and I looked at each other and shrugged. Neither of us could make any sense of why we'd stopped. Odds of an Oldsmobile's tires fitting a Plymouth were almost non-existent; so even if they lent us a jack we still didn't have a spare to put on. We watched through the brightly lit fog as Jere leaned down and looked in the driver's side window. He hesitated for a second and then knocked on the window with his right hand. Suddenly a head popped up in the backseat and then quickly disappeared again. Jere, wearing a big grin, kind of hopped back to the Plymouth. When he opened the door and flopped into his seat, he couldn't stop laughing.

"What's so funny?" RJ asked.

"Didn't you see that guy jump?" Jere asked back.

"Sure, but you didn't even try to talk to him."

"Start up the car RJ, he won't be helpin' us out."

"How do you know?"

"'Cause I seen his eyes, I seen what he was doin'."

"What's that mean?" RJ kept pressing.

"Shiiit, RJ, don't go gettin' dense on me. That boy and his girl just takin' a little break in the backseat to wait and see if the fog thins out."

"Oh," said RJ as he pulled the Plymouth back on to 71 and passed the parked Oldsmobile.

"They just doin' what everyone in this car like to be doin' right about now," Jere continued. "Gotta give 'em credit, they was under a blanket in the backseat; under a blanket of fog, on the side of Interstate 71. That takes a lotta nerve man."

"You mean, they . . ." Dango started to say.

Jere interrupted, "I mean exactly!" Then he started chuckling again. "His head popped up and he saw this big black dude lookin' at him. His eyes 'bout bulged out of his head. He dropped back down so fast and whipped that blanket over his head so quick, I didn't get a chance to say a word."

"Hey, you just lucky he didn't have a gun," RJ said.

"Oh, his weapon was out of the holster," RJ countered. "But he ain't gonna be able to fire it for awhile now."

"Jere, we got young boys in the car," RJ said through his laughter and tears.

Dango and I were cracking up, too. The banter of bad jokes and sexual innuendos continued for a good 10 minutes as we crept along 71, through the fog, on three good tires and one very worn rim.

About two minutes after the fun had died down, RJ broke the silence, "Hey, just saw a sign. Next turn off's Massillon/Mansfield, Highway 30. That's halfway. If there's gonna be anything open on this road, it'll be there."

"Halfway," I thought to myself. In eight hours since the Keller's had dropped us off we had only managed to cover 70 miles – 70 more miles to go. I remember actually thinking at that moment that I was in no hurry. I was in no hurry for this trip to end.

The last two miles to the Highway 30 turn-off did not "hurry" by. As RJ kept his focus on the road, the rest of us struggled to see if we could see any lights through the fog off the highway. With a mile left to go, we could make out the green vapor lights over the on and off ramps. As we headed down the ramp, we could make out a glow off to our right. Once we made the turn onto 30, we all let out a cheer – it was an open SOHIO station. RJ pulled the crippled Plymouth past the pumps, right up to the office and stopped. We all got out and stretched. There was one attendant on duty. He'd been sitting behind the desk reading something, but when we got out of the car he stood up. He was wearing dark green work pants, a short-sleeved SOHIO shirt and a baseball cap. He looked to be about the same age as Dango and me. My height, a face full of acne and a greasy red rag hanging out of the back pocket of the work pants. I figured him for a mid-Ohio farm boy who got the graveyard shift at the Interstate 71 midway SOHIO station for his summer job. And right now, he was looking from his well-lit, sparkling clean office, with a neat row of oil cans in the window, at probably the most unusual sight he'd seen all summer: Two giant black men, accompanied by two good-sized white boys, surrounding a beat-up '50s Plymouth with one very flat tire. You could tell he was sizing up the situation. I half expected him to lock himself in the men's room or go for the phone and call for back up. Instead he opened the door, came out and said, nice as you can be, "How you doing?"

"We got a problem," Jere said.

"I can see that," the attendant replied. "You got a spare?"

"Well, that's kind of a problem too," RJ added as he opened the trunk. "We got a few spares."

The attendant looked in and, even with our bags piled on top, immediately understood the situation.

"Drive it around back to the bay and we'll see what we can do."

He said "we" like he had someone else helping him, but I knew that wasn't the case. Maybe he meant "we" like the four of us would work with him; I didn't see much chance of that happening either. We followed RJ on foot as he "ka-thumped" the Plymouth around to the back of the station where the attendant had already opened one of the bay doors and turned on the service area light.

Jere opened the trunk again. Dango and I removed our bags and Jere started taking out the tires and rims. The attendant pulled out one of those hydraulic hand jacks, found a spot on the right underside of the Plymouth, and began to pump. The right rear tire lifted off the service bay floor and strands of rubber drooped down from it like blood dripping from type on a corny Halloween sign.

"My name's Abe," said the attendant as he worked. "You guys heading to Cleveland?"

"You're the man, Abe," RJ answered brightly. "You's really helpin' us out. I'm RJ, this here is Jere, Lee and Dango and we're all going to Cleveland. Didn't think we was gonna make it, 'til you came along."

"Hey, no problem," Abe answered back. "Nothin' ever happens here after three. Just keep an eye out for me to see if someone pulls up out front for gas."

"Glad to," said Dango.

"That's the last of those," Abe said as he spun the big four-prong socket wrench to remove the last lug nut. "I'll take what's left off the rim, but I'm not sure the rim's usable."

He walked the rim over to another machine, where he laid it flat and used a crowbar to circle the rim and pop off the destroyed tire.

"Better let me see those other rims," Abe said. "You got an inner tube?"

"Uh ohh," said Jere. "I don't think so."

"Well, I got one I think 'll work, but it'll cost five bucks."

RJ and Jere looked at each other. Apparently five bucks on a tire repair hadn't been budgeted into their trip.

"Dango and I got it," I cut in. "Five bucks for two to Cleveland's a good deal."

"Sounds good to me," Abe said. He walked over to a series of drawers along the wall of the service area and began going through them to find the proper size tube.

"I'm buying Cokes for everyone," Dango announced and headed for the big red Coke vending machine.

"Alright!" Jere shouted. "It's a tire changin' party!"

It kind of became a party, too; and Abe was the host and entertainment. The four travelers were the audience. We sat back and watched and clapped as Abe did all the work. And he was good. He found a new inner tube, put it in the best of Jere's four spares, then used the circle machine thing with the crowbar to get the new tube and tire on the best of the two rims, spread a little glue around the stem, filled it up with air, and then rolled it through a half tub of water to check for leaks. Every step of the way RJ and Jere would just tell him how great he was.

"How'd you learn to do that?"

"Man, you're good!"

"You should own this gas station."

"You wanna close up and come to Cleveland with us?"

At 10 minutes to 4:00 a.m., I looked at the big clock on the wall of the bay. Abe released the hydraulic jack and the Plymouth, with its new, or almost new, right rear tire was ready to go.

By that time, I think Abe was sorry to see us go. We all shook hands with him and then the four of us going in the Plymouth had to wipe our hands on some clean rags to get the grease off. As we were getting in the car, Jere suddenly stopped and said, "Hey, Abe needs to get something for all his work."

That caught Dango and me by surprise, because we'd already seen their hesitation over the inner tube we had ended up paying for. Silly me to think that Jere was talking about money. He went back, opened the trunk and took out one of the un-used used tires; then he got the old ruined rim and the destroyed tire shred. He somehow held all these in one arm and put his other arm around Abe.

"I hereby present these to you as thanks, and a token of our esteem, for the great service you performed for us here tonight." With that, he laid the offering at Abe's feet.

I, to this day, believe that RJ and Jere made that worthless gift to Abe as a true sign of their appreciation. It could very well have been perceived, I admit, as a sign of disrespect, a bad joke. But they had accepted Abe as a friend, just as they had accepted Dango and me. We were all unlikely players in this comical little scene that took place from 3:15 to a few minutes before 4:00 a.m. on a foggy, foggy night in nowhere Ohio. And each one of us had a blast being there. Abe certainly saw it the same way I did.

"I will cherish these gifts forever," he said, laughing. "Now get the hell out of here."

Back on 71, heading north to Cleveland, speed was still not an option.

"Damn, this fog is bad," RJ said. "I don't dare go much over forty."

"Might as well finish the vino, then," Jere chimed in. "There's enough left for one good drink apiece."

He took a healthy swig and passed the bottle back to Dango. Dango gulped some down and passed it on to me. This time I didn't even fake drinking, but handed it right back over the front seat to Jere. He gave it to RJ who, while keeping his eyes glued straight ahead to see as much as he could through the fog, polished the jug off. Jere rolled down his window and threw the empty half-gallon far off to the side of the interstate. We sure didn't have to worry about anyone seeing us litter – no one could see four feet from the Plymouth.

Shortly after that, Jere leaned his head back into the corner between the front seat and passenger side door and said, "Well, this is boring. I'm gonna get me a little shut eye."

He was right. Now that the car was fixed, the wine gone, and the novelty of the fog worn off, driving along at a slow 45 miles per hour was conducive to sleep. I looked over at Dango; he was already out. RJ was hunched forward keeping both hands on the wheel and keeping a sharp eye on what little road he could see in front of him. I, for some reason, was wide-awake. I'd had a Coke back at the mid-point SOHIO station, but I really hadn't had any sleep since the 20 or 30 minute nap under the tree in Illinois. We could pick up WJMO now on the radio. Every minute got us a step closer to Cleveland and the end of the trip. I didn't want to waste one second at the end of what I now saw in my mind as Dango and my modern-day cross-country odyssey.

I felt a slight jerk in the motion of the car. I looked up as RJ lifted his head quickly and shook it. I hadn't seen it, but I knew he'd closed his eyes for a second and his head had hit the top of the steering wheel. I could tell he was tired and fighting it. When he reached over to open the driver's side wind wing and held his face to the draft, that confirmed it. I was not going to allow a third accident because someone fell asleep behind the wheel.

"RJ!" I said loudly. "You getting tired? You want me to drive?"

"Lee," he answered, sounding surprised that someone was awake. I could see his head and shoulders raise up. "You okay, man? You feel like driving?"

"I'm wide awake, man," I shot back. "Pull over. I'll take it."

And he did just that. When the Plymouth came to a stop, he kicked Jere's foot.

"Jere, hop in back. Lee's gonna drive."

Jere got out his door, I got out mine and RJ slid across the front seat to the shotgun position. I opened the front and got behind the wheel. I had to move the seat up a bit. Jere got back in behind me and shut the open back door. Dango never even woke up. I put the Plymouth in gear, checked for any sign of lights behind on 71 and then started off.

"You okay?" RJ asked.

"Better than okay," I answered.

I kept the Plymouth at about 45 miles per hour and concentrated on the five to six feet I could see in front of the car. I stayed in the right-hand lane by watching the line in the middle of the highway. Everyone on 71 must have been doing the same thing, because I never came up on a car and no one passed me. Even the semis must have been taking it easy. I left the wind wing open just in case I did begin to tire, but I was enjoying myself. WJMO on the radio and another car full of sleeping passengers; I was the night pilot on the ship guiding my charges to safe harbor at home. The overactive romantic imagination of an 18-year-old in the driver's seat.

Bobby Bland came over the radio: *"I pity the fool . . . I pity the fool that falls in love with you."* I was "loving" this. I looked over at RJ. His giant head was back, his mouth open slightly and he was snoring softly like a little boy. In the backseat, Dango and Jere had somehow tipped together in the center. Dango's head was on Jere's shoulder and Jere's head rested in Dango's hair. I couldn't say both were smiling, but they were certainly sleeping peacefully. I looked at the fog in front of the car; it was still dense, but I could see it had gotten lighter. Somewhere the sun was coming up.

In August of 1964, Bobby Blue Bland had been the headliner at Gleason's. Everyone still called it Gleason's, even though they had sold out to The House of Blues in 1962. Dango and John AuWerter frequented the black club quite a bit that summer of '64, enough so they were recognized and didn't have to keep showing fake IDs. They were both 20 now, too, so they looked more like legal adults. When they went with dates they took a car, but when they went stag, to listen to the music and sit at the bar, they rode their Triumphs. John had purchased his Triumph in the summer of '63 to make sure he kept up with Dango when they went looking for trouble. They were "The Wild Ones" from the famous movie of the same name with Marlon Brando, of Shaker and Cleveland Heights.

After Bobby's first set ended, a little before midnight, and after seven or eight beers at the bar, John and Dango left Gleason's to go back to the Heights. It was a direct shot up Woodland Boulevard through the blocks of black Cleveland in the flatland to where the road started up the hill to the white suburbs.

At 55th Street, one of the major cross streets, the two bikers were stopped by a red light. The cross traffic, even at midnight on a weeknight, was quite heavy. The traffic heading up Woodland toward the Heights, very light as you might expect. Dango and John were in the first position at the 55th Street light waiting for it to change. Two big white guys, legs out on either side to balance their bikes, no helmets – 'cause you didn't wear helmets in the summer if you were just riding around town – waiting at the light. John was looking at the red light facing him, when he heard Dango kick his Triumph into first gear and accelerate. He looked over, mouth open, to see Dango try and shoot through the 55th Street cross traffic. He made it through a gap in the southbound cars, and John thought for a second he might clear the northbound too. And he might have too, except that a northbound '52 Chevy convertible with three young black guys saw him and accelerated and swerved to clip the Triumph's rear wheel. The impact knocked Dango and the bike down on its right side. It slid violently across the rest of 55th, sparks flying from the right tailpipe and handlebars, and slammed into the corner curb of 55th and Woodland. John watched as the Chevy continued north on 55th. The two guys who weren't driving looked back cheering and laughing. He had to wait a second longer for the light to change, before he could cross and get to Dango and the fallen Triumph. Dango had already gotten his leg out from under the bike and was standing next to it by the time John got to him. John helped him lift the downed Triumph and roll it out of the way of traffic. No cars stopped to see what happened. No cars stopped to help.

A few black teens from the neighborhood started to gather, but stayed on the sidewalk talking and laughing amongst themselves. John checked Dango out; his right arm was scraped and bleeding a little where the light jacket he'd been wearing had torn away. The right earpiece on his horn rims had broken off. Other than that, he was a lot better than he should have been. Before John could ask him why the hell he had run the light the cops showed up. A single patrol car with two white officers pulled up next to them on 55th. The two cops got out; the driver came over to John and Dango, while the other addressed the small crowd, "Okay guys, nothing to see here. Break it up. Go home."

"You guys alright?" the one cop said to the two "Wild Ones."

"Yeah, I'm okay," Dango replied.

"What happened?"

"Car clipped his rear tire when we were going through the intersection," John jumped in.

"Broke the light?" the cop asked.

"Guess so," John lied.

"Did you see the car?"

"No sir," Dango answered. "Happened so fast, they just kept going."

"You want to file a complaint?"

"No sir," Dango said. "I'm okay. The bikes just got a few scratches."

"Good!" the cop responded sharply. "Wouldn't come to anything if you did. What are you guys doing down here anyway?"

"We were at Gleason's," John offered. "Bobby Blue Bland's playing and we . . ."

"Okay got it," the policeman interrupted. "Now, listen up. Get on your bikes and hightail it back to the Heights, now. And a word to the wise, I wouldn't come riding your bikes down here anymore. We've found a couple of white bikers down here dead and dumped in alleys. This area's not safe. Understand?"

"Yes sir," they both answered.

"Now get out of here," the cop said, dismissing them.

Dango and John went back to their Triumphs and as John was helping Dango straighten his handlebars, he had his first chance to ask him, "What the hell were you doing, crashing that light?"

Dango put his glasses on with just the one earpiece and answered with a half-smile: "I thought it had turned green."

John never believed that answer, but that was the end of it. They kick-started their Triumphs and left downtown fast. It was also the end of Gleason's, or House of Blues, for the University School crowd. No one ever went back down from the Heights that we knew of. Two years later, in the Hough riots, the best black R&B club ever burned down.

I had never driven into Cleveland from the south before. As I approached on 71 in the Plymouth, the sun was trying to break through and the fog was beginning to dissipate. I decided to follow signs for "Downtown."

When I came to a bridge that I assumed was crossing the Cuyahoga River, the fog had cleared enough for me to make out the Terminal Tower, Cleveland's tallest building in 1961 and its central landmark. It faced directly onto Public Square, and from Public Square it was a straight shot up Euclid or Carnegie to the Heights.

I switched off WJMO and checked my watch. It was 6:15 a.m. I drove through Public Square and there was not a soul in sight, not even a bum. On the other side of the square I saw a large yellow street sweeper moving slowly along the curb. I headed out Carnegie east to the Heights and took a look at my passengers. RJ was still out next to me. In back, Dango and Jere had slumped back to their respective corners, but I could see that Dango's eyes were open and he was gazing at the silent city as we headed home in the half light.

"Hey," I whispered to get his attention.

He looked at me. He didn't say a word, but broke into that smile of his that said it all. I smiled back at him. We had come to the end of our journey and we had acknowledged to each other that we had accomplished something extraordinary.

When the Plymouth reached the bottom of Cedar Hill, where Carnegie turned into Cedar for the climb into the Heights, Dango and I woke the boys.

"Shiiit, we're here," Jere exclaimed as he stretched.

"We're on Cedar Road," I said to RJ. "You know Cedar Road?"

He looked at me and yawned.

"Dango's house is right up here, off Cedar," I continued. "Once you get back to Cedar, you'll be okay."

"No sweat," he said.

As the Plymouth climbed the hill, I remember thinking to myself, it was better we were headed to Dango's house than my house. Better to be dropped off in front of a modest wood frame house on a street of two-story wood frames than in front of a 30-room, three-story Tudor on two lots. Once I got started thinking like that, I got all mixed up. A second ago I had felt nothing but pride at what Dango and I had accomplished hitchhiking all the way across the country, and entering the great black city with two new black friends. We felt, for the ride anyway, we were so much like them and they were like us. And then to realize, with shame, that I didn't want them seeing my house, because they'd know in a second that we were nothing like them; that we had hitchhiked all that way not out of necessity, but for fun, for the adventure of it. We were children of privilege and that's what children of privilege did.

I turned on to Delaware, Dango's street, and all such thoughts left my head. When I came to Dango's driveway, I turned the Plymouth in, then put it in reverse, backed out into the street, then let it roll forward on the downhill slope and parked in front of the house. I even cut the front tires into the curb before I turned off the engine.

All of us exited the car and went back to the trunk. A lone paperboy, with his Plain Dealer bag over his shoulder, passed on the sidewalk, tossing the Saturday edition on front walkways. The thump of the papers hitting concrete or stone was the only sound in that silent early morning. Jere popped the trunk quietly, reached in and lifted Dango's bag out with difficulty. He handed it to Dango, shaking his head.

"Dango, you crazy man," he said softly. "You take it easy. You have a good life."

"I will, Jere," Dango replied. "You too. And thanks."

"Thanks for driving that last leg, Lee," RJ said as he handed me my bag. "I was beat."

"Glad I could do it," I answered. "Thanks for the ride. We'll never forget it."

"You boys take care," RJ said as he and Jere turned back to get in the Plymouth.

"Hey RJ," I called after him, as he was just getting into the driver's seat. "You guys have fun the rest of this weekend."

He got in, closed the door and through the open window looked back at me with a big smile, "No sweat, man, it's Cleveland!"

The Plymouth started to pull away down Delaware and RJ's big black arm came out for one last wave.

Dango and I stood in the road watching 'til they hit Cedar, then we turned, picked up our bags and started walking up the driveway to the house.

CHAPTER 11

Cleveland – January 1966

Once I left Cleveland, at the end of that summer in 1962, I made a break. Maybe I'd had enough beer; maybe I'd had my fill of small, grungy apartments; maybe I just realized my future was in another city, another state. Whatever it was, I left and didn't return again until January of 1966.

In those three and a half years, my only contacts with Dango were a few long distance phone calls and various strange postcards we would send to each other from time to time. I remember getting one from St. Petersburg, Florida in 1964, with a large orange and a girl in a bikini on the front. Message: "Better broads than in LA! Dango." I sent him one from Switzerland, where I went after graduating from college in 1965, with a picture of Lake Geneva and the Castle of Chillon on the front. Message: "Hitchhiking in Europe sucks! Lee." Even in correspondence, we didn't talk much.

How does one measure friendship, anyway? You don't keep score.

Though we hadn't seen each other in years, it never crossed my mind that Dango wasn't my best friend any more. I'm sure he felt the same way. I'd made lots of other friends in college in California, but they were "college friends", and somehow that meant they could not be as close as Dango and me. Our friendship had started in junior high school and grew throughout high school, when all things were possible for both of us. It was a bond formed before our minds began to close. A friendship never questioned, never judged, never analyzed. Two grown men can never form that kind of friendship; there's too much baggage.

What I did discover, however, was that I could now have that kind of bond with a woman. And that was the reason for my visit to Cleveland in 1966.

"He's here!"

Bob Lehmann shouted that as he held open the back door, from the kitchen to the garage, of his parent's home in Pepper Pike. The "he" he was referring to, of course, was Dango. Through the open garage doors in the dark driveway covered with snow, illuminated in the glow of the one spotlight shining down from above the garage, stood a motorcycle rider all dressed in black on a black Triumph. His hands were still on the handlebars, his legs spread to keep the bike up. The headlight was still on. He seemed frozen and ominous in that position.

I could understand the frozen part as I joined Lehmann in the garage and looked at Dango. He had just ridden over 100 miles, through a snowstorm, on a Friday afternoon and evening from Athens, Ohio to see me and the girl I was going to marry. We were having a party, a weeklong party and, like all the parties five years earlier, it was being held at Lehmann's house because his parents weren't home. They were in Germany visiting relatives for the holidays and they'd left Bob home to mind the house. Some things never change.

But everything else had changed. We were all now in our early twenties, graduated from college, taking those first steps toward assuming responsibility for our own lives. Everyone except Dango, who had one more year of undergraduate work at Ohio University in Athens to go; that was thanks to the one year he took off from college after his bathroom re-decoration at Rutgers.

The frozen black statue was alive. The right leg reached back and put down the kickstand of the Triumph; the gloved left hand turned the key and killed the engine. The bike came to rest on the kickstand, the left leg came over the bike and Dango started to clomp his way through the snow toward the garage where Lehmann and I stood watching his entrance. It was an entrance, too. I often wondered if Dango dressed like that on the bike because he knew the effect it had, or if he did it just out of necessity. Black lace-up combat boots, black ski pants, a black bomber jacket, thick black gloves, black helmet, and to top it off, a black scarf around his mouth trailing out from under the helmet in the back. The only sign of Dango you could see were the ever-present thick horn-rimmed glasses covering his eyes. I knew though, as he trod those last few feet into the garage, that he had a huge grin under that scarf. When he reached me, the giant black specter wrapped me in a bear hug and hoisted me off the cold concrete garage floor. I heard his muffled greeting through the scarf: "Livingston, you're here. Long time no see."

"Put me down, you big oaf. Get inside. It's freezing out here."

"California boy," Dango countered, laughing as he put me down.

Lehmann flipped a switch on the wall and the garage doors started to come down. Then all three of us headed to the kitchen, Dango taking off pieces of his costume on the way.

Once in the kitchen, Dango put his helmet, scarf and gloves on a chair, un-zipped his jacket and stomped his boots on a mat to shake off the remaining snow. Before he could take off his jacket, introductions had to be made.

"Dango, this is Jeanne," I said.

I was talking about the 5'7" young woman standing next to me. I wouldn't call her beautiful; she had short light brown hair, a slender body, a sharp-featured angular face and a lovely small mouth. The eyes were what got you. They were large, gray-green and they didn't miss a thing. We were standing by the small kitchen table with two chairs across from the door to the garage, across from the black be-decked motorcycle rider. Dango took one step toward us, picked Jeanne up and gave her a hug.

"Any girl that can love this guy," he said, referring to me of course. "Has got to be the greatest!"

"Dango," Jeanne responded laughing. "I've heard all about you."

She had, too. For a year and a half, I had told Jeanne Sullivan everything about Dango and Cleveland, everything about anything I thought was interesting in my life. I had met her at a party in Claremont, California in 1964, about two weeks before the start of my senior year and decided she was the girl I wanted to spend the rest of my life with. It took her a little longer to come around to that way of thinking, but then she was always a little smarter than I was.

I had heard about Jeanne since my freshman year at Claremont Men's College from the seven or eight local Claremont boys who attended the school. She lived in Claremont with her family and had gone to high school there. She had a "reputation." She had gone steady with a boy in the high school, and horror of horrors, slept with him. Not only that, but at the end of high school, she dumped him. That gave her the label of a "loose woman." But that wasn't the worst part of her reputation. She was also smart, some said brilliant. She had straight A's in high school and then received a full scholarship to Pomona College, the flagship and best of the five Claremont Colleges. She wasn't a virgin, she could talk, reason and drink circles around any of her high school classmates and she could have cared less what any of them thought about her. When I heard stories about her at CMC, it wasn't that they didn't like her; more that they didn't understand her. There was always a little awe in their voice when they spoke about her.

So when I saw her sitting on the floor, drinking a beer and smoking a cigarette at that party in someone's house in Claremont, I was already half in love with her. I wanted a smart woman; I was ready for a challenge. We had exchanged glances when I first came into the party. She had not seen me before and I could tell from those eyes that there was some curiosity. I had to figure out a way to "break the ice."

The opportunity came when the conversation among the 20 or so undergraduates turned to cars. Ford had just introduced their '65 Mustang model and, since that had been the "hottest" new car on the road for the last couple of years, it somehow warranted forty minutes of conversation time. Everyone in America seemed to have an opinion on automobiles and I guess it was a safe subject for everyone to talk about. I'd had a few beers and decided that if I was going to make an impression on Jeanne Sullivan, "safe" was not going to cut it. I plopped myself down on the floor next to her, my back to the sofa, looked over at her and said, "Talking about cars bores me to death."

She turned to me slowly and with a little smile replied, "Me too. What do you like to talk about?"

And so I launched into a conversation that would keep us both interested for 10 years – through the '60s into the '70s, at least, and that was no small achievement for relationships in those years. We talked about everything, we talked about nothing, and I kept up with her. We wrote letters to each other when we were apart. We could always laugh at each other. And we could always make love together. From that night in 1964, throughout our senior year, she at Pomona, me at CMC, we were inseparable. She helped me grow up. I got a single room, started listening to classical music and studied like I'd never studied before. I pulled my grades up to over a 3.0 for my four years at school thanks to my 3.8 my last year. Jeanne was *magna cum laude* at Pomona, majoring in Art History and already accepted into the graduate program at Harvard. I skipped applying to Harvard, but did apply and was accepted into the Graduate School at UCLA in Theater Arts. It meant for the school year of 1965/1966, Jeanne and I would be a continent apart. Not many of our friends, and certainly not our parents, gave the relationship much chance of lasting. We fooled them all and surprised ourselves. Meeting for semester break in Cleveland was the third time I had seen her that school year. We made a plan that once we had our MFA degrees after one year, we'd get married, live in Los Angeles and get jobs. It was still just a plan, still in the talking stages.

By the time Dango put Jeanne down they were fast friends. Dango, when he turned on the charm, could do that. But, before we had any chance to visit and talk, the "party" began in earnest. The word had gone out through the Heights, to all our US classmates that were in town, that Lehmann's house was open. After Dango's dramatic arrival, other friends began turning up every five minutes. By 9:00 p.m. there must have been 50 men and women in the downstairs area of the house. You could tell everyone was growing up, because they brought their own liquor and it wasn't all beer.

At 1:30 a.m. the party started to wind down. Jeanne came to me and said she was tired and going upstairs to bed. Lehmann had given us his parent's suite for the week; I walked Jeanne up, gave her a kiss good night and then went back downstairs to find Dango. Eight or nine hard partiers were left in the living room, so Dango and I took a couple of beers and went back to the kitchen. We fell into our easy pattern of talking just as we had talked every evening at Sequoia or at the Mayfield corner bar. This evening, we had more to talk about – four years of life to cover. Dango started it off with a compliment.

"Jeanne's special, Lee. You're really lucky."

"Believe me, I know it. She's become my best friend. I talk to her and tell her everything like I used to talk to you."

"Yeah, I don't know what we said to each other, but I miss it. Since you left and I got booted from Rutgers I don't even have AuWerter around anymore, either."

"No close friends at OU?" I asked

"No, not really," he answered. "A few girlfriends – met a new girl this year."

That's how the conversation went for a while, each of us filling in the gaps in the last years. Both of us had the same experience with male friendships; we had made friends with other guys in college, but the high school bonds remained the strongest. I have a hunch that's true of most men growing up in the United States. Before and during high school American males are still open; once they head off to college, a door shuts, and ambition, competition and distrust take over. I guess you could call it a loss of innocence, but the years from the end of summer in 1962, when I had last seen Dango, to January of 1966 when he appeared out of the snow at Lehmann's, loss of innocence applied to the entire country.

It was as if history had been asleep in the fifties, and now in the early '60s had awakened angry and was ready to give us a kick in the teeth. From the Cuban missile crisis, to JFK's assassination, to an exploding conflict in Vietnam, to black riots in cities across the United States, Dango and I discussed how each had affected us in the last three years. Those were the big, general topics we talked about. But finally, around 2:45 a.m., Dango got to what he really wanted to tell me.

"You know, I got engaged in 1963."

"What!? I never heard about it."

"I know. I was going to tell you about it, but it all happened so fast," he went on. "You remember, Karen Fielder, the girl from Cleveland Heights High? I took her out a few times in the summer of '62."

I did remember Karen. In fact, Dango had made me find another place to sleep one night when we were sharing the sleeping hole, because he had a date with her. He dated her a few times that summer, but I had never known it was serious. She had drinks with us once or twice at the Mayfield corner bar and had come with a contingent of Heights High School girls to the big backyard bash that had ended the summer of '62.

I remembered that she was blond with a great body, alert eyes and a sharp tongue. A girl that turned you on and intimidated you at the same time. Or maybe that was just my impression. I always thought my kind of girl was the shy, quiet type. I could fantasize about sleeping with a Karen Fielder, but I always thought she'd hand me my head on a platter afterwards. Obviously she wasn't like that, or if she was, it never bothered Dango. Obviously I'd changed too, since I had a strong, intimidating girl waiting for me upstairs.

"You and Karen Fielder were gonna get married? What happened?"

"My parents wouldn't have it. We were too young."

I interpreted that the minute I heard it, as "My mom went ballistic!"

And I heard later, that's exactly what happened. Once again Dango's mom knew what was worst for him. But at that moment, I was more interested in hearing about his relationship with Karen since I'd never known Dango to get serious with a girl.

"So, how did you guys get so close?" I asked. "You actually got engaged?"

"Hey, had an engagement party. Set a date in 1964. Karen had her picture in the Plain Dealer."

"Tell me." I was astounded. Jeanne and I hadn't done anything that formal.

"I was really bummed out when I came back here after Rutgers. I thought I'd blown it. My mom constantly told me I'd blown it. I ended up renting a small apartment to get out of the house and re-started the tree service to make a little money. But none of the guys were around and it was lonely, man. I gave Karen a call one weekend. She was home from Miami of Ohio, where she went to college, and we started going out again. I mean, right from the beginning, she was great. She just turned me around. Told me I could do anything. Kicked me in the butt for being down. On weekends she couldn't get to Cleveland, I'd go down to Oxford, that's where Miami is. I mean we had a real boyfriend-girlfriend thing going on."

"And just a little sex thrown in?" I said with a smile.

"All the time," he said back with a smile. "And it was the best. Wanna know why it was the best?"

"Sure," I said. But I thought I had a pretty good idea why.

"After we'd make love, we'd lie around and talk and laugh and then make love again."

"That is the best," I said. I thought to myself, though, this sure doesn't sound like Dango; he's growing up or he's still in love with her.

"I called her Kare, she called me Bo. No Dango, just Bo."

"Sounds great, Dango. When did you guys decide to get married?"

"Late '63, after she came back from Europe."

"Why didn't you go to Europe with her?"

"Money. I didn't have enough and summer was the best time to make it cutting down those elms."

"Makes sense."

"We were in love, Lee. And we were a lot the same. Her parents drove her crazy, but they loved me. I couldn't wait to get away from my parents, but they sure didn't love her. It was simple, really. We talked together. We drank together. We laughed together. We slept together. We cursed the dark together. And then she got pregnant."

"Why didn't you tell me that to begin with?" I said. "That's why you guys decided to get married."

"Not really," Dango added. And then after a beat, "It wasn't mine."

Now I knew I was never going to get to sleep. I stood up, went over to the refrigerator and opened it.

"Want another beer?" I asked Dango. "All that's left in here is Carling's Black Label."

"Sure, why not."

I took two out, shut the refrigerator door, found a church key on the counter and opened both cans.

"Here," I said, handing Dango his can. "Now, explain it to me. This I got to hear."

What I heard told me things about my friend that I had never known. I had seen him at times as wild, impetuous and foolish. I had also seen his softer side, when he was kind and caring to his friends and strangers. I loved both sides. I had never known, however, that he could be close and loving with a woman. It certainly had never happened in high school and I always suspected, because of his relationship with his mother, that forming a close bond with any woman would be difficult for him. What I had heard so far about Karen Fielder made me think that they were good drinking, fucking buddies to help each other get through the mid-college years. It was much more than that.

In the late summer of 1963, Karen had gone with three girlfriends from Miami of Ohio on a six-week tour of Europe. Traveling through Europe in those years was wonderful for Americans; it was cheap and Europeans still appreciated us for saving their ass in World War II. Three young, pretty American college girls, tooling around with Eurail passes and a little money to spend, were sure to have a good time. At least Karen didn't get drunk and have a wild night of amore with an Italian waiter. The unfortunate affair did happen in Rome, however. The girls met up with some frat boys and jocks from Miami of Ohio on their own excursion in Europe. Karen got drunk and had a night of passion with a good-looking forward from the Miami basketball team. Did she think of her big boyfriend with the horn-rimmed glasses back in Cleveland before she succumbed to temptation? Probably, for a moment, but 1963 was the very beginning of the "love the one you're with" era, so, what the hell. The trip was a blast, she returned to Ohio, her boyfriend and the first semester of her junior year. Dango had enrolled at Ohio University, so they had an inter-state school romance. In late September, the bill for Karen's European transgression came due – she missed her period.

There was never any question whether or not to have the baby. Karen didn't love the father; she loved Dango. Female children of privilege in those days either married or had abortions when faced with an unexpected pregnancy. Fortunately for Karen, her Miami basketball player came from money and would pay for her abortion. They got the name of an "abortion clinic" in Covington, Kentucky, just across the border from Cincinnati, from the forward's black fraternity house boy. With that kind of recommendation, what could go wrong?

Karen had the money from her one-night-stand and didn't want anything more to do with him. She had made a mistake and would handle the consequences by herself. Her bravado lasted up until three days before her appointment in Covington, when she broke down on her every-other-night phone call with Dango.

"When she told me what happened and what she was going to do, she was sobbing," Dango said. It was still very early morning in Lehmann's kitchen. "She thought it was the end of us. I just said, 'I'll be there for you. I'll take you to Covington.' And that's what I did."

I guess that was the kind of friend I always knew Dango was, for a man or a woman. I looked at him and could see he was choked-up remembering that call. It was the only time I can remember him crying except for the night in the snow bank at Coolidge's. I sat there kind of choked-up myself, wondering what I would have done if Jeanne had ever told me she was carrying another man's baby.

"So then, you asked her to marry you?"

"Yeah, I decided I wanted to marry her on the ride down to Covington."

"How come?"

"I just realized I wanted to be with her, take care of her, but not because she was weak or helpless or anything like that, more because she was so strong, or trying to be so strong. I gotta tell you what she said to me on the trip down there that really capped it for me."

I waited.

"I'd ridden my bike over to Oxford from Athens and then I drove her Ford to Covington. I mean, we had handwritten directions to this place in god-knows-where part of Covington. She's being the navigator. We're going to an abortion clinic for god's sake, doing something totally illegal in another state. I'm scared for her, I'm a little scared period, and she just wants to get it over with."

"So we're crossing the bridge over the Ohio from Cincinnati to Covington. It's night, of course, they don't do these things during the day, and it starts to rain. Not just a little storm, one of those big, bucket-of-water-per-second storms, and we're trying to find a small street in a town I've never been in and never want to be in again."

"Anyway, I can hardly see a thing, it's pitch black, pouring rain, I sure as hell can't see street signs, so I get a little panicky. I start swearing and talking out loud, 'I can't see the signs. Show me a sign! Let me see a fucking sign!'"

"Karen, who's on the way to her own abortion for god's sake, gets fed up with my ranting and raving. She looks over at me and says, 'You want to see a sign? You want to see a fucking sign? Here's a sign!' I look over at her and she flips me off."

"She gave you the bird?"

"Yup. Flipped me off for being such a hysterical asshole. It was perfect. We both started to laugh so hard, we 'bout peed in the car. That's when I knew I loved her and wanted to marry her. That's what I meant before when I said 'curse the darkness together.' You hit rough times, you give it the finger and drive through it."

"Jesus," I said. "You should have married her!"

"Yeah, I know," he replied. "Wasn't meant to be. The abortion was awful by the way. Turned out not to be a clinic, but the doctor's house. He did it out of his back room. Had his degree on the wall from some medical school in a college I'd never heard of. On the way back she started hemorrhaging and I took her to an emergency room in Cincinnati. Her mom had to come up from Florida, and they wouldn't even let me in to see her."

"And you still asked her to marry you?"

"Right before Thanksgiving, when she was all better," he said. "Her parents always liked me and once they found out I wasn't the guy who got her pregnant, they were all for it. Helped us make plans and everything."

"All for it," I thought. They must have believed that they were getting a saint for a son-in-law. Anyone who loved their daughter that much, who wouldn't want him in the family?

"But my mom was right," Dango went on. "We were way too young. Neither of us was even twenty-one."

"Where's Karen now?" I asked.

"Getting her master's at Kent State. She's married."

"Too bad," I said, and I meant it. After a while it was clear that there was nothing more to say. "I'm heading up to bed," I said. "We'll talk more in the morning."

"I'm beat, too," Dango said. "I'm crashing on the couch in the living room."

I woke up at 11:30 the next morning to the smell of bacon frying. I threw on a loose sweater over my T-shirt and pulled on the same pair of jeans I'd worn the day before. I headed down to the kitchen. Jeanne and Lehmann's girlfriend, Janet, were busy making bacon, eggs, and hash browns for a late breakfast. Lehmann had a large plastic garbage bag and was roaming the house picking up stray paper and plastic glasses, discarded empty beer cans and liquor bottles. He also emptied all the full ashtrays into the same bag. Another sign the US gang had gotten older – everything else in the house was in good order, nothing spilled, nothing broken. No one was trying to be particularly quiet, but neither the girls cooking nor the junk landing in Lehmann's bag woke the big lump on the couch. Dango was on his back, mouth open, peacefully snoring. When the girls signaled me breakfast was ready, I went over and kicked his foot to wake him as I had done countless times at Sequoia and in the sleeping hole. He sat up, yawned and stretched. He was only wearing underwear. I threw him his black ski pants.

"Here, get dressed. Breakfast's ready."

"What time is it?" he asked.

"Almost noon."

"Shit! I'm gonna have to take off in a couple of hours."

"You can't stay tonight?"

"Nah. I've got an advanced calculus final Monday. I'm gonna have to cram all day tomorrow. Can't do that here, that's for sure."

I was stunned how conscientious Dango had become. What happened to the old "in 20 years" motto? It also meant, of course, that he had made the 200-plus miles round trip to Cleveland through a snowstorm, on a motorcycle, just to see me and meet my girlfriend. I thought about saying something to him about that, but knew he'd only shrug it off. He had never considered not coming.

Breakfast was a big hit. Lehmann made Bloody Marys for all of us and the three males told some of our old high school and Cleveland exploits. Jeanne hadn't heard about Dango bouncing the rock off my head or how I had set the one-day record for demerits at University School. The way the five of us got along, I found myself wishing that Karen Fielder had been there for Dango. I'm sure from what I'd heard about her, she would have loved hearing the story of Dango in the backseat of Ron's Cadillac. I wondered if he'd told her that one.

Jeanne amazed me. One minute she'd be discussing some esoteric, intellectual thing with Lehmann, the next minute telling Dango a dirty joke. Maybe there is something to be said for a Harvard education. Two hours flew by and we never even got out of the kitchen.

Lehmann and Janet finally broke it up when they left to go into town and do some grocery shopping. I gave them 20 bucks for Jeanne and me. Dango stood up from the table.

"I better get going," he said.

"Look Dango," Jeanne said. "Why don't I say 'goodbye' now? I have to run upstairs and place a collect call to my parents in California."

She walked over to him and gave him a big hug.

"You're a wonderful friend to Lee," she said. "You better come out to California."

"I will," he said. "You take care of him."

"I don't think it's supposed to work that way," she said, smiling as she left the kitchen. "He's supposed to take care of me."

I followed Dango back into the living room and sat in one of the plush armchairs as he began to put on his winter riding gear.

"So the hitchhiking in Europe last summer wasn't that good?" he asked.

"Pretty shitty," I answered. "I stuck a little American flag on one bag and a sign that said 'Students' on one of my pal Tony's. We met in Luxembourg and hitchhiked up through Germany to Denmark and Sweden. Germany wasn't bad, but we ended up taking trains in the Scandinavian countries and it rained all the time in Sweden, too."

"Maybe it was the American flag?"

"Maybe, but the Germans were cool. They were real friendly. I'll tell you where you'll never get a ride – Switzerland. We tried getting to Geneva from the German side. Four hours, not one car even slowed down!"

"It's pretty much over in the states, too," Dango added. "I hitched back and forth to Rutgers a bunch in '62 and '63, but now, with most of the interstates completed, you just get short piddly rides."

Dango finished lacing his boots, stood up and began gathering the rest of his gear.

"Have you heard from AuWerter?" I asked.

"He joined the Army."

"AuWerter!? The Army!?"

"Yeah, when he graduated from Rutgers he lost his deferment and you know how he has always got everything worked out. He volunteered for the Army's officer candidate school so he could choose his own combat branch. He signed up for armor. Told me,

'I never saw a tank in all the news footage from Vietnam, so I figure I'm safe.'"

"Actually, that sounds pretty smart," I said.

"I thought so too," Dango went on. "But he's already through basic training and he's in advanced officer training at Fort Knox and they've been told that once they're through, half of them will be assigned to infantry."

"You mean he could still end up in 'Nam?"

"Yep, he's sweating bullets, pardon the pun."

"What are you going to do about the draft?" I asked.

He had slipped on his thick bomber jacket, wrapped his scarf around his neck and picked up his helmet and gloves. We continued the uncomfortable conversation that all males in their twenties were having during the late '6os as we headed for the door to the garage.

"I've got a semester left to figure it out. What about you?"

"My brother works with an editor at CBS who's a captain in the Army Reserve," I replied. "Might try that."

"Jesus, that's a six-year commitment."

"Yeah, but if Jeanne and I get married, at least I won't get shot."

"That's true."

We entered the garage. Dango must have moved the Triumph in sometime during the night. He hit the switch to open the garage door. It was about as nice a day as you could expect for Cleveland in late January – very cold, but the sun was out and there wasn't a cloud in the sky. He placed his gloves on the bike seat, zipped up his jacket and started to put on his helmet. Before he got it up to his head, I caught his arm.

"Hey, thanks for coming."

"Anytime," Dango said.

We had another of our awkward man hugs; he put on his helmet and straddled the Triumph. While he was pulling on his gloves, he threw out the final challenge.

"You invite me to the wedding, I'll be there."

"You got it," I said.

He kick-started the Triumph, revved it a couple of times and took it slow out of the garage onto the snow-covered driveway. At the street, he stopped, turned and waved, then was gone in a second.

He didn't end up coming to the wedding. It was a small family affair in Carmel and we really didn't invite anyone. I didn't get an invitation to his wedding, either. He married an Ohio University girl he met that last semester. They moved to Philadelphia. I did join the Army Reserves before my wedding in 1966 and went to basic training in April of 1967 at Fort Leonard Wood. Dango somehow got into the Marine Reserves in Pennsylvania and did his basic at Camp Lejeune in 1968.

How we kept in touch the six years until I saw him again, I've forgotten. I know it wasn't postcards. A letter here and there? An occasional phone call out of the blue? Hearing about each other through the old high school grapevine? Christmas cards? Whatever it was, we always knew where the other one was – a phone number, an address. What we didn't know, was how the other one was.

I never went back to Cleveland after meeting Jeanne there that semester break in 1966.

I never wanted to go back after the last time I saw Dango in 1972.

CHAPTER 12

Los Angeles – Christmas 1972

A t 2:40 in the afternoon on December 24th, 1972, Robert T. Lyons, Jr. knocked at the door of Jeanne's and my old Spanish-style house in the Hollywood Hills. When I opened the door, I didn't recognize him. I still saw Dango.

I could certainly be excused for seeing my old best friend; the big shit-eating grin was still there; he still wore the thick horn-rimmed glasses. But the clothes should have tipped me off: I was looking at a new man. He was wearing a clean, freshly pressed, blue-check Brooks Brothers' buttoned-down shirt, new khaki slacks, and expensive dark brown loafers. In each hand he held a large Bullock's department store bag filled with brightly wrapped Christmas presents. You could tell by the wrapping paper that many of the gifts had been wrapped by hand.

Dango had moved to Long Beach, California from Philadelphia in the spring of 1972. He had graduated from an Eastman Dillon brokerage-training program at the top of his class and as his reward he was given a choice of brokerage offices where he could start work. He chose Long Beach. He had married in December of 1968 to the girl he met at OU. It ended in divorce in the fall of '71 in Philadelphia. He decided to make a break with the East when he signed on with Eastman Dillon. He was going to start fresh in California: finally getting away from his family, his failed marriage and the "old school" Eastern ties. He wouldn't be completely alone, however: he did have a "best friend" that lived in Los Angeles.

With Dango's arrival, that meant my two closest friends from University School had moved to California. Lehmann had shown up in Los Angeles in 1968 with his new wife, Janet, in tow. I never asked either of them why they had come to California, but Jeanne swore my presence had something to do with it. She insisted I gave them some sense of security. I'd be there for them like their families weren't. Trouble was, I wasn't there for myself.

I grabbed one of Dango's gift bags and escorted him into the big living room with a large bay window looking out over Beachwood Canyon. Off to the right you could see the famous Hollywood sign. Jeanne came up from the downstairs, where the bedrooms were, and welcomed him with a big hug. She then sat with him by the big Noble fir Christmas tree and helped him place the presents he had brought under the tree. I went into the kitchen, opened two Czechoslovakian Pilsner Urquell beers, and brought them back to the living room for Dango and myself. James Taylor, Carman McRae, and one of the Beatles' white album LPs were stacked and playing on the stereo. It was the start of a picture-perfect Christmas.

Jeanne and I sat together on an old antique couch we had reupholstered, facing the Christmas tree. Dango sat in a Morris chair to the side of us, his new loafers propped up on a small ottoman, beer in his hand. *Fire and Rain* was playing on the stereo; *"Well, there's hours of time on the telephone line to talk about things to come . . ."*

"Ya know," Dango said. "It's 76 degrees outside."

We all looked out the window, past the Christmas tree, at the perfect LA day. Since we were facing west there was no smog.

"I've never had a Christmas when there's never been snow or it hasn't been freezing."

Jeanne smiled at him. "You'll get used to it," she said. "The winters in Southern California are the best."

"Jeanne and I always pray for rain on New Year's Day," I chimed in. "Everyone watching the Rose Bowl back east won't pack up and move out here."

The minute I said it I regretted it and tried to take it back: "That doesn't apply to you, of course."

Dango laughed at my discomfort.

"Good one, Lee," he said. "You keep forgetting I've been here over six months now."

I didn't keep forgetting it. I just never thought about it. I was 29. It was a time of my life that I was really into me. Dango had arrived in California in June and I had only seen him one other time before his Christmas visit. He had spent a Saturday and Sunday with me at the house in July. Jeanne had been on a trip back east on business for the art museum. She was already an Associate Curator for Modern Art. I was keeping up with her. I was an Associate Creative Director at one of the largest advertising agencies in town. In the six years we'd been married, we'd risen fast in our chosen professions, bought our own house in the Hollywood Hills and both drove Porsches – mine a '67 911, Jeanne's a new mid-engine 914. I'm surprised the LA Times hadn't featured us as one of the hot, young, up-and-coming Los Angeles couples of the '70s yet. Maybe The Times could spot the handwriting on the wall. Our marriage was hanging by a thread and the two of us were holding on to each other to try and save it.

Dango knew it. The weekend in July he came up to see me, we double-dated with one of the creative department secretaries, and I took out one of the media girls. We took them to drinks and dinner at the old Hollywood Brown Derby, a restaurant Jeanne and I never went to, and then back to the house for a nightcap. While Dango had a brandy with the secretary in the living room, I took the media girl downstairs. At least I had the decency to bang her in the guest bedroom. I was kind of upset that Dango hadn't scored with his date, since she had slept with most of the guys in the creative department.

"I'm sorry I haven't called you more," I said, responding to Dango's statement. "Jeanne and I have been really busy."

"That's okay," Dango answered. "It's been hectic for me too, getting accustomed to the new job. You know, I have to get up at 5:00 a.m. to get in before the market opens."

"What's that like?" Jeanne asked.

Dango started in on a long description on the life of a young stockbroker in a new office. I listened but wasn't really paying attention. I remember he mentioned two hours of cold-calling to try and find new clients and having to study different mutual funds so he could know which ones to recommend to different investors, but I tuned out. I had never had much interest in the stock market or finances. I saw myself as a creative type and now people were actually paying me to create things. So what if they were only slogans, or headlines or jingles – the money was outrageous. I'd even been paid $2,000 for working on a freelance account and coming up with a billboard headline for a new Japanese plum wine – "Plum Good!" $1,000 a word in 1972 – who said writing didn't pay.

Since I wasn't listening to what they were saying, I found myself watching Dango and Jeanne and coming to the realization that these were my two best friends. I loved them both, they knew more about me than any other two individuals, they were my closest companions, and yet I was unfaithful to my wife and hadn't bothered to call Dango for six months when he was in nearby Long Beach. What did that say about me?

"You okay, honey?" Jeanne said.

"Fine, why?" I answered.

"You look like you were tearing up."

"I'm just happy my two favorite people are gonna be here for Christmas," I said. It was an honest answer but sounded a little trite coming from a dishonest "creative."

Jeanne stood up. "Well, you and Dango catch up. I've got to go finish that article for Art Forum."

She left us to go back to the small office we had off the kitchen. She still had her small Corona typewriter that she'd had at Pomona and Harvard. Art Forum paid her $250 for reviews of artists showing at Los Angeles galleries. The art world had a long way to go to catch up to the advertising freelance pay scale.

"You okay?" Dango asked.

"Yeah, I'm good. It really is good to see you."

"No I meant you and Jeanne. Are you guys okay? You know, the last time I came up here...?"

Good old Dango, cut right to the point. No bullshit. I looked at him and lied.

"Oh yeah, we're fine," I said. "That other stuff doesn't mean anything."

Jesus, there I was in 1972 talking to Dango, who I still considered my "closest" friend, and that crap came out of my mouth. If only I could have frozen that moment, taken it back and talked to him like I might have talked to him while drinking beers some afternoon by the Chagrin River. He reached out to me to help me – because I was lost and he recognized it. I didn't see it, though. I didn't see that maybe he was lost too and we could have helped each other. I didn't see that maybe he had come to the realization that his defiant credo – "In 20 years will it make a difference" – was a joke. Life progresses each day no matter how many beers you drink to try and slow it down. And what you do one day makes a difference the very next day. The problem is you don't usually realize it makes a difference until those "next days" pass and turn into years.

Dango got it, I didn't. The funny thing, or maybe a sad thing, was that while Dango was starting to question his nihilist credo, the whole damn country had adopted it with gusto. Once the Vietnam War really got going, and then when King and Bobby Kennedy got shot, a lot of America's younger generation began to believe that whatever you did didn't make a difference at all, much less in 20 years. Not everyone became a hippie, but with new, easy access to pot and birth control pills, everyone's attitude about almost everything became a lot more "laid back." Dango trying to get serious and start a new life in Long Beach was bucking a trend.

Carefree Lee, on the other hand, with success, money and a Porsche in the garage was a '70s cliché. Sure, I loved Jeanne, but these were the years of "free love." Actually, it should have been called "free sex" because love had nothing to do with it. All those tortuous hours I'd spent in high school and college trying to talk and charm a girl into bed had been wasted training for the '70s. Now I could get laid if I had a couple of hours to spare after a party, or a lunch, or a Los Angeles Advertising Softball League game. The women, many of them smart and lovely, didn't care that I was married. And, apparently, neither did I. I was young, drinking too much and I knew that it wouldn't make a difference. I thought I could always change when I needed to, but I wasn't really thinking.

Dango put his beer down and looked over at me.

"You know, I had a close call in '71?"

"What do you mean?"

"I totaled my Triumph and broke my arm."

"I do the advertising for Honda motorcycles," I told him. "You ride bikes a lot, sooner or later, you're gonna get in an accident. Car drivers just don't see you half the time. Did someone hit you?"

"No, it was my fault."

"You hit someone? You dropped the bike on a curve?"

"No. I hit a wall."

"You hit a wall?"

"I was on my way back to Philadelphia from my two week Marine National Guard summer camp at Lejeune and I lost it. I blacked out. I was in the middle of nowhere, it was night, I went off the road into one of those picturesque fieldstone walls in Virginia. They said I must have been going 70 when I left the road and hit the damn thing."

"Jesus. Had you been drinking?" I asked.

Dango laughed. "That's what they asked me at the hospital when I came to. No, I hadn't been drinking. They checked."

"So what – you just fell asleep?"

"Kinda. I was really depressed and angry."

I looked at him. He wasn't looking at me, but past the Christmas tree again out at the Southern California afternoon. It dawned on me that this was some kind of a confession to an old, best friend. I wasn't prepared for it and I certainly wasn't qualified to give him any advice.

"What got you so mad?" I asked.

"I had these buddies I met in basic that were sent to Vietnam," he said.

"From your Guard unit?"

"No, regular Marines. I knew 'em from basic. I found out one of them was already killed."

Guilt was not an unusual emotion from National Guard or Reserve soldiers during the Vietnam War years. When you joined the National Guard or Reserve, you made a commitment for six years, but in the '60s and '70s it was used as a way to escape being sent to 'Nam. I was able to join an Army Armed Forces Radio-Television Unit from Van Nuys because my brother worked with a Captain in the unit. The unit was all white, except for one black NCO. Out of a roster of 30, we had two actors on TV shows, three talent agents, two journalists, three film producers and a couple of lawyers. I was the only ad guy. Years later, one of the lawyers became head of a studio and one of the journalists became a famous film critic on a morning network TV show. Every guy in that unit thanked his lucky stars every day that he managed somehow to find this way to serve his country and avoid the draft.

Dango's Marine National Guard service was in a Quartermaster unit, not nearly as cushy as Armed Forces Radio-Television, but never likely to be called to active duty in Vietnam. The guilt came every evening when you'd watch the news and see the fighting in Vietnam. When the casualty figures came up, you'd turn away from the screen. Those guys fighting were there in your place. Once again, children of privilege had found a way to avoid responsibility.

"Hey Dango," I said. "All of us feel a little guilt that we're not over there. And most of us are angry 'cause it's such a shitty war, one we shouldn't be fighting, but you can't let it get to you."

I was trying to sound reassuring, but it was really a conversation I didn't want to have. Where the hell was my old "devil-may-care" buddy Dango?

"I know, I know. But in '71, I was down anyway," he said. "In '71, I could tell the marriage was beginning to go south, I was refurbishing townhouses in Philly and that was leading nowhere – and then the shit about my buddies from the Marines – I just lost it."

I was afraid I knew where he was heading and I really didn't want to go there but I asked anyway, "Whattya mean?"

"I mean, I'd taken an entire bottle of sleeping pills, before I got on that bike."

"Jesus, Dango. You were trying to kill yourself?"

"Pretty half-assed job, huh?" he continued. "I told you I was depressed. Anyway, I went back to Philly, got a divorce, sold the townhouse, talked to my sister who set me up with a good shrink, and here I am a new man with a new job in a new place."

That was enough for me. He'd dealt with it, and he was fine, let's move to safe ground. "So that's why you ended up coming out here?"

"Isn't that why everybody comes out here?" he said, laughing.

"Well, it's definitely not Cleveland," I said.

"Not Philly either," he went on. "Long Beach is great. I'm doing good at the job. I go running on the beach. I think I'll buy a sailboat."

He was keeping busy, I thought to myself. I wondered if those were instructions from his shrink. Had he taken care of his demons?

Had he talked with his shrink about his mom?

"Want another beer?" I said, standing up.

The rest of that day passed without incident. After another Pilsner, I took Dango for a walk up on a bluff just across the street from our house. There were five empty, steep, vacant lots that faced the street on one side and Griffith Park on the other side. From the top, on a clear day, you could see all the way across Los Angeles to Long Beach. After a rain, you could even see Catalina. This Christmas Eve day we hadn't had any rain for a while, so you could see downtown and over to the Baldwin Hills, but the smog made anything past that blend into the haze. Dango loved the view anyway.

"God, it's enormous!" he said.

"As far as the eye can see," I responded. "Few more years, it'll go all the way to San Diego."

"But you and Jeanne get to live up here above it all."

"Yeah, if only that were true," I said chuckling.

We went back to the house. Dango went to his room so he could relax a little and clean up. I went to the kitchen and put a leg of lamb in the oven for our dinner. Jeanne and I were the modern two-job couple; we shared the cooking assignments. At 5:30 we met back in the living room for the cocktail hour. That was a holdover tradition from our 50's parents. I was excited to introduce Dango to something new.

"Wait until you try this," I said.

"What?"

I went to the refrigerator freezer and pulled out a fifth of Bombay gin. Jeanne brought three Martini glasses we'd put in the freezer earlier and a jar of olives stuffed with pimentos.

"Gin?" Dango said. "You drink martinis now?"

"Not just any martinis," I answered. "These are special. One of Jeanne's wealthy, older art collector buddies showed me how to make 'em."

With that I poured the partially-frozen Bombay into the chilled glasses, added the olives and then from my pocket, I pulled out a small spritzer bottle of Martini & Rossi Vermouth. One quick spritz in each glass and I passed one to Dango and one to Jeanne. It was still the first few months of my "martini career" so I still shuddered when I took my first sip and felt the cold warmth start to enter my body. Dango took a sip and almost choked. He put the glass down on the coaster on the coffee table.

"Out of my league, Livingstons," he sputtered out. "Give me another Pilsner Urquell. Quick."

We all laughed and I went to the kitchen and got him his beer. I finished his Martini after I finished mine.

That evening and the following Christmas Day were idyllic. The laughter, the talk, the closeness between the three of us, whether alcohol aided or not, were non-stop. Dango still had that magic to draw you in and make you feel comfortable. What was really magical was how he somehow brought Jeanne and me closer together that Christmas, too.

I've forgotten what I gave Dango for a gift that Christmas. I don't remember what he got for Jeanne but I'll never forget what he gave me. It was one of the only boxes in his bag of gifts that wasn't hand-wrapped. It came from Brooks Brothers and when I opened it, I was looking at a classic blue-striped, button-down shirt accompanied by a very conservative blue-and-red thick striped tie. It was a shirt and tie my dad or his dad could have worn when they went downtown to work in Cleveland. It was a shirt and tie that the account executives at my advertising agency would wear with the suits they wore every day. The head of our agency had a phrase to sum-up what kind of man would wear a shirt and tie like this: "Solid guy, solid tie."

It was, of course, the wrong gift for me. Or was it? I think Dango had thought long and hard about that Brooks Brothers ensemble. It was a message gift to his old best friend – stop fighting it, take responsibility, be a man. It's what he believed he was doing in Long Beach.

I got up from where I was sitting to unwrap my gifts, walked over to Dango and gave him a hug to thank him. It was a sincere hug, not so much for the gift, but because I was truly thankful that he had come to spend Christmas with us.

He left early afternoon Christmas day about the same time he arrived the day before. Jeanne and I walked him to the car and helped him load his gifts and bag. We stood by the gate and watched as he turned the car around in the street to head back down the hill and on to Long Beach. We all gave quick waves. It had been a great three-person Christmas.

Jeanne went back to the office to finish her article for Art Forum. I cleaned up around the tree and loaded the breakfast dishes in the dishwasher. Everything went back to normal – for a while.

I don't recall talking to Dango once in 1973. You'd think since we were so geographically close one of us would have at least called the other a couple of times. When we lived on either side of the country, we kept in touch two or three times every year. I didn't know how busy Dango was or what he was doing with his free time. I didn't bother to find out either. I just knew I was busy pursuing my advertising career and being careless with my marriage. Jeanne became a personage in the "Art World." We saw each other weekends and evenings. We attended fewer and fewer functions together.

It was an early evening in August 1973 when Lehmann called. I remember Jeanne and I had changed into shorts and light short-sleeved shirts to try and stay cool. The Santa Anas were blowing; the heat stayed in the city and the smog hung over the ocean.

"Lee," he said. "Dango's dead."

He didn't have to say any more, but he did. He told me he had gotten a call from AuWerter in Cleveland, who had gotten a call from Dango's father in Florida. The two friends living closest to him were the last to find out.

I knew the second I heard he was dead how he had done it. It wasn't going to be sleeping pills or running his motorcycle head on into traffic. No, he would put a gun in his mouth and pull the trigger. That's exactly what he did.

CHAPTER 13

Then to Now

"*Wish I didn't know now what I didn't know then.*" Sometimes I think that all the truths about life are summed up in Rock 'n' Roll lyrics. I always loved that line from Bob Seger's *Against the Wind*. No matter how old you are when you hear it, you feel so much wiser "now" than you did back "then."

Now they call it bi-polar. Back then, it was called manic-depressive. Doesn't make any difference what they call it; I didn't know that was what Dango suffered from until just recently. For 30 years after his death, I didn't want to know anything about it. I was angry. I was helpless. I felt some guilt because I had been absent for him in the last few years. So I used his death as an excuse to cut off all ties to Cleveland and those old high school friends. If there was any one person to blame, I was pretty sure I knew who it was then, and what I've learned since only tends to support that belief.

Dango's mom was diagnosed as a manic-depressive and, in fact, institutionalized twice to combat her sickness. Despite what she must have learned about herself, it didn't stop her from trying to ruin Dango's life. She was responsible for breaking off the engagement to Karen Fielder. She actually had a doll made of the girl Dango did marry to stick pins in. She belittled and berated him for years and they had knockdown screaming fights. I knew, or thought I knew, that he couldn't stand her, even that he hated her. Perhaps it's part of the disease, to find out which one of your children is the most susceptible to it, and pass it on. One thing is certain, neither Dango nor his mother could ever really see the damage, because their "love" was too strong. Far from hating her, he loved her and sought her love and approval 'til the end. I know now, that he never stopped writing her endearing letters, with detailed financial advice, telling her how beautiful she was and how much he loved her. Every Valentine's Day, Mother's Day and Birthday, he sent her a cute, funny or touching card. Each letter and card was signed "With love" or "Your loving son." And she saved and cherished them all 'til the day she died – which was February 27, 2010.

What does that prove? Only that with all I know now, I don't know much more than I did then. I had always assumed that Dango had killed himself because he couldn't find love. Maybe it was just that he couldn't recognize it. Maybe that's what he inherited from his mother.

But he was loved! I had thought that, because of his relationship with his mother, he might have a hard time relating to other women. Karen Fielder to this day calls him "the love of my life." His wife said he was a responsible, caring, loving husband and that it was her immaturity that caused their separation. In his last months in Long Beach, he had a steady girlfriend who wrote to his parents after his death about how much she loved him and how wonderful he was. It turns out that Dango had no problem loving women and having them love him in return.

For 30 years I pictured his time in Long Beach as a final depressing chapter in his life: a dingy apartment, few friends, and an unfulfilling job. Maybe I did that to try and feel better about myself, because his best friend in high school just ignored him. I was wrong again. He shared a bright apartment right at the beach with another broker from Eastman Dillon; he was one of the leading producers in the office and, besides the girlfriend, he had a close group of friends that adored him. He did end up purchasing that sailboat, by the way, and used it to take those friends out sailing and partying.

His openness, his ability to make almost everyone he came in contact with feel good about themselves, and feel comfortable with him, continued right to the end. It was a gift he had. A gift which everyone who got to know him saw, and loved about him. But, along with that gift, came a curse that none of us saw. A despair so deep that Dango only glimpsed it a few times – in a snow bank at New Year's Eve, at a busy intersection in Cleveland, in a bathroom mirror at Rutgers. Each time alcohol probably helped darken his vision, until finally, alone in the apartment in Long Beach, it was too black.

Dango left no note. I never expected one. I knew how he made decisions, good or bad. He made them quickly, acted on them and never looked back. The very first time I knew Dango was going to be my best friend, before he was called Dango, he made a decision like that. And I was glad he did.

It was in the summer of 1956, between the 7th and 8th grades, and there were four of us from Roxboro Junior High riding our English bikes that day. English racing bikes with their thin tires and multiple gearing had just become the rage. All the kids in the Heights had one. I had a brand new one; Dango's parents had bought him a used one they had refurbished. Two other buddies, Rich and Frankie were riding with us and, since it was summer and we weren't in camp, we were bored and looking for something to do. Bob, of course, came up with the idea – we'd ride through Lake View Cemetery.

Lake View Cemetery was the dowager queen of Cleveland cemeteries. It was home to the burial plots of Cleveland's rich and famous and boasted the gravesite of James Garfield, one of Ohio's eight Presidents. All that meant nothing to four 13-year-olds who simply wanted bike paths with a steep grade so they could go fast and lean dangerously into curves. Lake View was perfect for that. As the name suggests, it was situated on the slope between the Heights and downtown Cleveland, and in the 19th century, before the city built up below it, it must have had a beautiful view of Lake Erie. It was a giant cemetery and the roadways dividing the various gravesite sections curved along and down the hillside.

We entered Lake View from an unguarded entrance off of Mayfield Road in Cleveland Heights and on the first run through followed Dango. The ride down on the English bikes was thrilling for 13-year-olds. Dango would build up speed then cut across on a side road to another road heading down. We zigzagged and sped our way to the bottom in what seemed like seconds, laughing and shouting all the way. We spotted a few workers but since it was early afternoon on a summer weekday we didn't seem to bother anyone. Lake View may have been built to store bodies, but to our way of thinking, it made an excellent bike park.

Once we hit the bottom of the hill, we exited the cemetery at the main Euclid Ave entrance, then cut around to Mayfield for the climb back up to the Heights. Mayfield curved and formed both the southern and western border of Lake View. Mayfield on the western side ran through a small picturesque area of shops and restaurants, known as Little Italy, before it began its steep climb up to the Heights. Still excited and energized after our first run, we quickly took Euclid back to Mayfield and, dropping our bikes into low gear, made short work of the uphill climb.

The second run through Lake View was even more fun than the first. We were more familiar with the course and went even faster. This time Rich and Frankie took the lead because, if truth be told, they were the better riders. Bob and I had both had growth spurts between 12 and 13 and at 5'10" we were two of the biggest kids in our class. Rich and Frankie were at least a half-foot shorter than we were and probably a half second quicker with their reflexes. They cut the curves sharper and loved beating the "big guys" whenever they could. All of us were fearless.

Climbing up Mayfield Hill took a little longer after the second run but it didn't dampen our enthusiasm for a third race through the old cemetery. The third run turned out to be the most fun of all, because some official at Lake View must have heard about the speeding bike racers and sent some guards out on the roadways to intercept us. Old men on foot trying to stop kids on bikes with a built-up head of steam must be like trying to catch hummingbirds without a net. We all split up, took different roads, and blew by any guards standing in our way with a quick jog left or right. At the Euclid gate, they had one guard waiting to block us; we zipped by him like Bugs Bunny past Elmer Fudd. I was the last one out and I swear I saw him spinning.

Riding along Euclid back to Mayfield we were laughing so hard we were crying. We knew, however, that was the last run of the day. Heading up Mayfield the lighter Rich and Frankie pulled ahead of Dango and me. Still not completely competent with my gearing on the new bike, I accidentally slipped into a higher gear, had to stop, shift to a lower gear and slowly begin pedaling again.

Dango had pulled ahead of me about 100 feet up the hill. I was looking down to make sure I stayed in the right gear and pedaling as fast as I could to keep climbing when I heard trouble.

"Hey! Where are you going?" a voice shouted from right in front of me.

I looked up to see three kids who looked to be a few years older than I was, standing right in the middle of the sidewalk blocking my way. The kid in the center, the ringleader I guess, put out his hand and grabbed the handlebars of my English racer. I put my feet on the ground and looked at the boys in front of me. I was a little bit scared and a little bit pissed. Young teenagers from the Heights had little practice with confrontation.

"Where do you think I'm going?" I said, trying to sound tough.

"This is Little Italy. You Heights babies shouldn't be down here."

Of course, they were from Little Italy, I thought. They were walking clichés of what we called "Italian greasers." Each of them had long black "greased-down" hair, dark T-shirts and, I swear to God, the leader holding my bike had a pack of cigarettes rolled up in the left sleeve of his tee. I kept up the tough act.

"So, get out of my way and I won't be down here."

With that, he took his free hand and hit me hard on the shoulder.

"Shut up, butt fuck." Then, he looked down at my new bike and said "Nice bike."

I was scared now. The tough boy act was about to end with either me crying or peeing in my pants. Then I heard:

"Is there a problem here?"

Dango had come back down the hill and pulled his bike next to mine to face the greaser. The wannabe hood took his hand off my handlebars, but didn't move and still blocked our way.

"Great. Now we got two 'Heights' pansy boys."

"You wanna keep talking or do you want to fight, small stuff?" Dango said coldly.

I couldn't believe Dango had said that. I also couldn't believe that Dango had noticed that, even though these guys may have been older, they were actually a couple of inches shorter than we were. The hair just made them look taller.

"Come on, four eyes," the greaser said. "Get off that bike. I'll fight you!"

Bob had those big old horned rim glasses even in seventh grade. He leaned down to start getting off his bike and whispered to me, "Follow me, quick."

He turned his bike facing downhill like he was going to lay it down on the sidewalk and then, suddenly, when he had both his feet free of the bike, his right leg shot out and he kicked the "leader of the pack" right in the groin. Then, in a split second, Dango hopped on his bike and started pedaling furiously down Mayfield back toward Euclid. I flipped my bike around and was right behind him. The mini Mafia boys were stunned for a few moments and their leader was doubled over. So, by the time they started to run after us we could look back and laugh. We kept laughing all the way down to Euclid, over to Cedar Hill and back up into the Heights. We went back to the Berkshire house and that was the first night Dango ever slept over.

Getting out of Little Italy that day was sort of like getting out of the train yard in Clovis five years later. But that's what Dango and I did, that's what defined our friendship – we were there for each other; we got each other out of scrapes.

When we set off in the Star Chief that summer of 1961, Dango and I didn't take a camera with us. When you're going to live forever, taking pictures seems like a waste of time. So, I have no photos of us in the Pontiac with the top down, or at the market in Sequoia, or in front of the Lido de Paris in Las Vegas. I don't think Jeanne and I took a picture even when Dango came to spend Christmas with us in the Hollywood Hills. In fact, the only pictures I know of the two of us are two photos that were in the University School 1961 Yearbook. One a shot of the two of us coming in the front door at Coolidge's New Year's Eve Party; the other a shot of us with our heads bowed saying grace before a University School lunch. Under that one, someone thought it would be funny to put the caption: ". . . deliver us from evil." I think that was a reference to my "fuck you all" acrostic in the school paper, although one of our classmates might have had a premonition. There's a terrific picture of Dango and AuWerter in Rutger's T-shirts standing in front of Demerest Hall – must have been the start to freshman year.

I only saved one piece of memorabilia from the five-day trek cross country and that was the ESSO map of the USA I bought in Las Vegas and kept in my back pocket during the trip. I ended up throwing it out when I left the Hollywood Hills house in 1978, four years after my marriage to Jeanne had ended. We separated at the end of '73 and divorced in 1974. It was an amicable divorce arranged by her lawyer/father. He structured it so I could keep the house for a very fair settlement. When Los Angeles real estate skyrocketed, it turned out to be better than fair. Jeanne moved on to Washington D.C. and became the director of a large museum. I stayed in Los Angeles and became a Vice President/Creative Director at the city's largest ad agency.

When I finally packed up and moved from the Hollywood Hills house, I remember going through a box of old high school and college papers I'd saved. I carefully picked out the worn and yellowed ESSO map and started to spread it on the floor. It fell apart at two of the folds. I could see where I'd drawn in the time zone lines and I could still see some of the marks and scribbling I'd added when I got back to the house in Cleveland. I had used the map when I finally confessed to my parents one evening about the hitchhiking. They ended up being thrilled with the story when they saw how it had affected me. By Joplin, Missouri, I'd drawn an arrow and printed the name "Reola." By Clovis, I'd written "Santa Fe Bull!" Just outside of St. Louis, I'd marked where Dango went off the road. For each long ride, I'd put down the names of the people who had picked us up alongside the highway line. I studied the old decaying map for about five minutes, thinking about Dango, before I threw it out.

I wish I had that map now. I wish I had a map for all the trips I've taken in my life. Because looking back, that's kind of the way I break it down. Life, I mean. I see it as a series of many different journeys searching for love, or purpose, or God, or maybe just a friend to kick back and talk with who doesn't judge you – and those may all be the same thing. I wish I could show Dango some of the roads I've taken, places I've been and people I've met since he left. I wish, most of all, that he were here to see his old friend, remarried, father of two boys, accepting responsibility. I even wear Brooks Brothers' shirts now, though still without ties. I remember Dango on that hillside in Illinois playing with the Keller kids and I wish that he could have had kids of his own. I think that might have saved him.

All I know for sure is that in the summer of 1961, I pulled him off a rock in Sequoia. He never let go and dragged me on a road trip out of adolescence. It was the shortest, most intense and most powerful of all my life journeys and it was an experience that could only have happened then, because not only were the two 18-year-olds changing every day – so was the country. It was just before the interstates, the death of JFK, Vietnam and race riots. Gas was 28 cents a gallon and people opened the doors of their Chevys, Cadillacs and Plymouths to two strangers, invited them in and helped them get where they were going.

Acknowledgments

In the fall of 2009 I took a course in memoir writing through the UCLA Extension taught by Jennie Nash. Due to Jennie's encouraging, no-nonsense teaching style, by the end of the class I had completed my first chapter and a solid chapter-by-chapter outline for the rest of the book. I also had a mentor and critical editor to keep me going. Without the guidance from such a fine and accomplished author, *In The Rearview Mirror* never would have hit the road (www.jennienash.com).

During 2010, I made contact with a few old friends of Dango's to help me fill in the holes in my recollection. Foremost among these was John AuWerter, Dango's old Rutgers roommate and other best friend from University School. His help, fact checking and adding his stories about Dango were essential to completing the book. His wife Deborah also helped critiquing and fact-checking the first draft. They even made a trip to Cleveland and took a picture of the sleeping hole apartment.

In the late summer of 2010, I visited Dango's sister in the Philadelphia area, Diane Dunning, and she graciously provided me with family details in the story of his relationship with his mother. Two other old friends from Dango's high school and college days provided stories and glimpses of his personality that were invaluable – special thanks to Carol Wilder and Lee Geis.

Along with Jennie Nash, my wife Linda read every chapter as I finished them and made corrections and comments. She's the world's best 5th grade teacher and I could not have finished *In The Rearview Mirror* without her support and encouragement. Michèle Hermet's help with editing and formatting was also invaluable.

As I stated in the narrative, I did not take any pictures during the summer journey of 1961. I also did not take any notes. These stories are as I remember them looking back 50 years later. I have tried not to enhance or diminish their importance. The passage of time took care of that.

Lee Livingston

About the Author

Lee Livingston was born in Los Angeles, California, and spent his early childhood in New York City and most of his school years in Cleveland, Ohio. He graduated from Claremont Men's College in 1965 with a BA in Literature and finally completed his MFA in Theatre Arts from UCLA in 2005. He was a Vice President/ Creative Director at Grey Advertising in Los Angeles. From 1980 until the present he has been running his own commercial film production company in Los Angeles. He lives in Los Angeles with his wife and two sons.

Go back in time, follow the route, see the cars and the pictures at:

intherearviewmirrorbook.com

Made in the USA
San Bernardino, CA
28 May 2018